The Most Important Question

WHY JESUS?

The Most Important Question
WHY JESUS?

DAN JASSMAN

The Most Important Question: Why Jesus?

Unless indicated, all Scripture references are taken from The Holy Bible: English Standard Version. (2016). Crossway Bibles. Used by permission. All rights reserved. All emphasis in Scripture quotations have been added by the author.

For more information, email danjassman@gmail.com.

ISBN: 979-8-89694-279-5 - eBook

ISBN: 979-8-89694-280-1 - Paperback

Dedication

I want to dedicate this book to my wife, Amanda, and the church I serve, Network Bible Fellowship. Never in my wildest imagination would I have considered writing a book without their encouragement and support. For years, they urged me to consider this endeavor. I repeatedly pushed it aside, intimidated by the idea of becoming an author.

However, Amanda would not let it go. Without her encouragement, support, and blessing, I would not have taken this step. She helped me see how this work could reach a broader audience and, hopefully, make a lasting impact on those weighing the question of *Why Jesus?* or simply wanting to understand their faith better. Likewise, Network Bible Fellowship is a great church that allows me the time to dig deep to teach the truth.

Ultimately, I want to dedicate this work to Jesus, Who is the subject of this book. As a child, I would have said, "I believe because my parents believed." However, as I studied, learned, and examined the evidence, I came to believe because I believe. Without Jesus, my life would not be the same, and I desire to give Him all glory and honor—something that I pray this work will do.

Table of Contents

Preface

Thank you for trusting me enough to pick up this book. I have always been fascinated by logic, reason, and the evidence highlighting faith as a reasonable position rather than wishful thinking. This interest led me to apologetics, a fancy term for exploring the evidence and reasons we have for faith. This field of study seeks to answer the hard questions and demonstrates that contrary to some opinions, faith is not a blind leap, but a reasonable step based on evidence.

Toward the end of 2017, apologetics was laid on my heart as the focus for my sermons for 2018. I dug into many resources for topics, ideas, questions to address, the evidence available, etc. The first sermon was determined by a question I posed to an atheist I knew, "What is your biggest hangup to faith?" Her response was, "Hypocrisy in the church." I knew then that this would be my first sermon, with many to follow. This book is drawn from research and study done over that year and my nearly thirty years of pastoral ministry.

I addressed many topics throughout 2018, this book focuses on the most important. Why Jesus? I may have grown up in a pastor's home with a faith perspective, but this is not the case for some of the sources found in this book. Some of them began as atheists, seeking to disprove the Bible, but through investigating the evidence for the Bible, and especially

Jesus, their journey brought them to faith in Jesus. I have tried to write in a way that is understandable to the seeker, who knows little to nothing regarding Jesus, but also to help the believer better understand the faith they profess. Only you can determine if I accomplished that goal.

We live in a time and age where the idea of truth has been jettisoned. The pursuit of truth sacrificed for the pursuit of consensus. One religion is as good as another, or none at all. It doesn't matter what you believe if you are sincere in your belief, whatever it may be. However, that line of thinking is self-defeating and frankly dangerous. History shows that sincerely held but incorrect beliefs have caused great harm. Consider the medical practice of "bloodletting," where blood was drained to cure disease but weakened the body's ability to fight disease. Or the devastation of things like slavery or the witch trials when people sincerely believed but were sincerely wrong in what they believed. For years my wife didn't feel well despite what we believed to be healthy eating. She found out that she had a gluten intolerance. Reality didn't care what we believed—she suffered the consequences of a wrong assumption. What you believe does matter because it guides and shapes how you behave, and there are consequences for getting it wrong. Ask anyone who believed a con artist only to find themselves conned. If Jesus is Who He claimed to be, then there is nothing more important than what you believe about Jesus. The underlying questions are, "What did He claim, and do you have reason to believe it?"

I have divided this book into two parts. Part 1, "Foundations for the Reasonableness of Faith," lays the groundwork and foundation for assumptions that will be taken up in part 2, *Why Jesus?* Before narrowing the focus to Jesus specifically, it is necessary to establish the reasonableness of faith in God in general and the Bible as a trustworthy source. I am not exhaustive in the case that I make but rather seek to provide an adequate basis for the reasonableness of faith, and more specifically for faith in Jesus.

I pray that you are blessed in the journey and that if you are in the place of asking, "Why Jesus," you may end with "Why not," convinced by the evidence at hand. I have chosen to capitalize pronouns that refer to Jesus or God, except for where I am quoting from a source that does not. Hopefully, by the time you finish your reading, you will understand why I prefer to use capitals in referring to Jesus as I lay out scientific, historical, philosophical, and logical cases for why Jesus is more than just another option.

If you already believe in Jesus, I pray that you are encouraged and strengthened in your pursuit of knowing Him more deeply and walking with Him more faithfully. If you are new to this information, I pray that you may come to a greater understanding of why it is reasonable to put faith in Jesus and to follow Him because what you believe does matter, and in this case, eternity may hang in the balance. So, let's get started.

PART 1

FOUNDATIONS FOR THE REASONABLENESS OF FAITH

Chapter 1

The Fallacy of Straw Man Arguments

Matthew 7:15-23
"Why would I believe in a God Whose
followers don't even follow Him?"

Excellent question. If you are asking it, or would like an answer, this book is for you. One of the primary objections to Christianity is hypocrisy in the church. Behind that objection often lies personal pain. But does the behavior of Christians—whether good or bad—tell us anything definitive about the existence of God?

WHEN ARGUMENTS MISS THE MARK

Once while searching for sermon illustrations, I recall reading of a neighbor who wanted to borrow a lawnmower. The neighbor, however, responded that he was unable to loan out his lawnmower because a particular flight was delayed. Of course, this was nonsense, so the neighbor asked what on earth a delayed flight had to do with him borrowing the lawnmower.

The neighbor replied, "Nothing. I don't want to loan you my lawnmower and one excuse is as good as another."

Perhaps you have heard of straw man arguments. A straw man argument is when someone misrepresents an idea to make it easier to argue against. It works like this: instead of addressing the actual position someone holds, you create a distorted, simplified version—a 'straw man'—that is easier to knock down. This creates diversions that avoid engaging the central question. Many reasons people cite for not believing in God fall into the category of straw man arguments.

- "Religious people are hypocrites."
- "Christianity has been responsible for violence and oppression."
- "I've been hurt by the church."
- "Religion is just a tool for controlling people."
- "God can't exist because of evil and suffering."
- "I can't believe in God if there is a hell."
- "It's exclusive to believe Jesus is the only way."

Each of these objections may identify genuine problems but notice what they have in common: none directly addresses whether God exists. They're critiques of religious institutions and people, not arguments about the existence of God. They attack the straw man, not the real question. When examined closely, these arguments don't hold up—they're more like excuses than logical reasons not to believe. Like the lawnmower illustration, they are not as much logical arguments against the existence of God as excuses not to believe.

Back in 2018, I felt led to focus my sermons on apologetics. Apologetics is simply a fancy term for defending the hope you have and the faith you hold. Many books make the case for God, which I do not plan to replicate here. However, in making our case for Jesus you must begin with the existence of God. While I do not plan to address all the straw man arguments used as excuses for not believing in God, I will begin with perhaps the one that many see as a nail in God's coffin, so to speak. Before starting my sermon series, I spoke with a self-proclaimed atheist, and I asked if she could help me out. I told her that I wanted to address problems people had with believing in God and if she would share with me her number one reason for not believing. Without missing a beat, she said, "Hypocrisy in the church." What she failed to realize is that Jesus also had issues with hypocrisy and that hypocrisy is a straw man argument that has nothing to do with whether God exists. Like the lawnmower, hypocrisy has been used by many to dismiss God but is completely unrelated to whether God exists.

SEEING THE ENTIRE FIELD

After doing premarital counseling on my own for years, my wife Amanda had this novel idea. What if we did premarital counseling together? Our first test case was a Christian couple from a different church, who were between pastors at the time. The idea was that Amanda would bring a different perspective, likely one that was better than mine. Especially since Amanda and I are about as opposite as you can get.

We gathered in my office for our first session. They were agreeable to Amanda joining in. Nonetheless, what was fascinating about this first premarital counseling session was it converted more into Christian counseling. Both individuals were believers and had been in the church for many years, but he confessed that he was struggling with his faith because of what he witnessed in the church. He emotionally quipped, "I see how they are on Sunday, but I also know how they live the rest of the week." He was and is a believer, but like many unbelievers, hypocrisy had become a stumbling block to his faith.

It was one of those moments when I believed God gave me what I said next. He and his fiancée were both farmers and I asked him, "When you look over your fields, what stands out, the crops or the weeds?" He didn't miss a beat, "The weeds!" Isn't it interesting that a farmer can have acres upon acres of good crops, yet will become hyper-focused on the patch of weeds in the middle? The one area somehow missed by Roundup. The problem isn't the existence of weeds—there will always be weeds. The problem is that the weeds divert attention from the healthy crop.

Think of the church in the same way. Jesus told a parable where He spoke of the wheat and the weeds, which may be tares depending on your translation, growing together (Matthew 13:24-30). "Weeds" rivet our attention, but don't diminish the reality of the "wheat"; flaws within the church don't undermine the truth of Christianity, nor those authentically living out their faith. For whatever reason, the negative captivates our attention. People want to look at the bad that has been done as an argument against God while ignoring all the good. The presence of "weeds" doesn't change the reality that the "wheat" remains, and in far greater abundance if honestly measured.

WHAT ABOUT THE WHEAT

Barna group research in 2007 revealed that many who reject Christianity do so not because of the evidence, but for other reasons. You are back to the straw man arguments. "Not because of the evidence." Not because there is a reason not to believe, but because they view Christians as 1) anti-homosexual, 2) judgmental, and let's not forget 3) hypocritical.[1] Critics like Christopher Hitchens have famously opposed Christianity viewing "religion as poison," and Steven Weinberg said, "Good people will do good things bad people will do bad things, but for good people to do bad things—that takes religion."[2] These are good soundbites. Of course, their next step is to point out all the evils done in the name of religion throughout history. But are they accurate representations or merely constructions of 'straw man' arguments? Such critiques may highlight actions done in the name of Christianity, but soundbites, like weeds, exist within a larger context. These critics fail to differentiate between actions that contradict Jesus' teachings and those that reflect them, relying on a highly selective reading of history. This isn't to dismiss or excuse wrongdoing done in Christ's name. Rather, it's to place it in proper context and proportion, as even secular historians acknowledge Christianity's valuable impact and cultural influence.

What about all the Christians who were bad people doing bad things who became good people doing excellent things? What about the benefits produced by Christianity? Ironically, the *rationale* atheists employ against God can be flipped into an argument against atheism—atheism has caused more deaths than religion.[3] A great number of people have died from medical malpractice, but *most* people don't stop going to see the doctor just because bad doctors exist. Whatever philosophy, religion, institution, or category you examine,

---

1   Clark, Mark. *The Problem of God: Answering a Skeptic's Challenges to Christianity*. Grand Rapids, Michigan: Zondervan, 2017, p181.
2   Ibid, p.182.
3   Examples would include Joseph Stalin, Mao Zedong, Pol Pot, Kim II Sung, and Enver Hoxha.

there will be both "wheat" and "weeds," yet some choose to use it as a straw man argument against God.

In Luke 9:51-56, Jesus is traveling to Jerusalem with His disciples when a Samaritan village refuses to welcome him. James and John were infuriated, and religion of course being the root of all evil, Jesus has them gird on their swords to teach them a lesson. Wait a minute, that isn't what happened. James and John *wanted* to call down fire from heaven, but Jesus *rebuked* them. Atrocities or evil done in the name of Jesus that contradict the teachings of Jesus don't change the reality of Jesus. As Augustine said, "We are never to judge a philosophy by its abuse."[4] Christianity doesn't rise or fall with Christians but with Jesus Christ.

The presence of "weeds" is not an argument against the reality of "wheat." As historian Alister McGrath observes: "One of the greatest tasks confronting the church today is to rescue Christianity from misunderstandings."[5] Just because a perception is present doesn't make it true. How often have you jumped to a conclusion only to later learn it was wrong? First impressions are often wrong impressions because you do not know what you do not know until you acquire more information.

HIJACKED PERCEPTIONS

It hit me when I was out running. One mile is 5,280 feet. How often is that true? Is it true whether I run on Monday, Wednesday, or Friday? Is it true when the sun is shining? Does the distance of a mile change when it is overcast, or worse yet,

---

4   https://quotefancy.com/quote/905829/Saint-Augustine-Never-judge-a-philosophy-by-its-abuse
5   McGrath, Alister. *Mere Apologetics: How to Help Seekers & Skeptics Find Faith*. Grand Rapids, Michigan: BakerBooks, 2012, p11.

raining on my parade? One mile is, always and forever, 5,280 feet. Yet, I have used a Fitbit with GPS for years, and it doesn't always measure a mile the same. Despite running the same route, one day my mile marker is in one place, another day in another. What changed? It wasn't the distance of a mile. The weather conditions influence and affect the ability of the GPS to read accurately the distance leaving it with approximations, a "perception" that is sometimes accurate and other times greatly misses the mark.

The teachings of Jesus have not changed, but our interpretations of them have. As people look back over history, they often see not the teachings of Jesus lived out as much as Christianity under the overcast of political and cultural influences that have adulterated the Christian faith, blending values Jesus never intended. Just as my GPS can falsely read a mile many have misperceived Christianity due to not being able to separate what was true from that which was politically motivated and misperceived as Christian. Christianity has often been judged based on where it has been abused rather than evaluated considering where Christians have authentically lived out the faith. Jeremiah Johnston wrote a book called, *Unimaginable: What Our World Would Be Like without Christianity.* I highly recommend it if you want to explore the positive impact of those who genuinely follow Jesus.

For many their perception of Christianity has been distorted, in part, due to a failure to understand history. Namely how Christianity got absorbed into and hijacked by the Roman empire, which as a "Christian" empire, did the same thing as the Roman empire did before. You can examine many battles that were ascribed to Christians or religions that were not religious in nature or motivated by faith but rather politically driven. You have likely heard the saying, "You can't judge a book by its cover." If you look more deeply you will discover that much done in the name of God had nothing to do with God but political and cultural forces instead.

Mark Clark commented,

> In fact, if one adds up all the deaths during the Crusades, the Inquisition, and the witch trials across both Europe and the Americas we find that 'Christians' killed between 200,000-250,000 people over the course of 500 years [this is far less than Dan Brown's claims in the DaVinci code for 5 million women killed in the witch hunts over four centuries, which historians estimate at 40,000-60,000]. And we must recognize that many of these [200,000-250,000] were killed in the context of warring armies between nations.[67]

Much of this history is used to discount Christianity and the existence of God, but it has nothing to do with religion or whether God exists. Clark continues,

> If we look at the past hundred years, the most violent and horrific regimes humankind has seen have been atheistic, not religious. Joseph Stalin's Russia, Mao's China, the Khmer Rouge in Cambodia, and of course Adolph Hitler's 'final solution' in Europe were all driven by communist, Marxist, and atheistic philosophies that rejected

---

6   Clark, Mark. *The Problem of God: Answering a Skeptic's Challenges to Christianity.* Grand Rapids, Michigan: Zondervan, 2017, p193.
7   Ibid, p.193-194.

organized religion and God as a central tenet of their system of belief.

Atheists may look at hypocrisy in the church or violence done through history as an argument against God, while ignoring that it can just as easily be flipped to an argument against atheism. It is a straw man argument that doesn't hold up, like the lawnmower and the flight, they are unrelated matters. People's perception of Christianity has been hijacked by events that were not reflective of Jesus but politics. Instances when the "church" has failed to follow the teachings of Jesus are hardly an argument against God in general or Christianity specifically. It merely reveals the fallenness of humanity. Those who use these details against faith are generally atheists who point out the wrongs done by the church, and there were and continue to be wrongs done by the church, but they ignore the last 100 years where atheism has done far more damage than anything Christians have done. As Alister McGrath recognizes: "The twentieth century gave rise to one of the greatest and most distressing paradoxes in human history, that the greatest intolerance and violence of the century were practiced by those who believed that religion causes intolerance and violence."[8]

Consider a parent and a child. A parent teaches certain values to their children. If a child chooses not to live by those values, it does not disprove the existence of the parent. It only speaks of the character of the child. People's perception of Christianity has been hijacked by events that were not reflective of God or Jesus but mere politics. Unfortunately, people have selectively chosen the worst examples from history to say that it is wrong to believe in God because look at all the

---

8   McGrath, Alister. *The Twilight of Atheism: The Rise and Fall of Faith in the Modern World*. Colorado Springs, CO, 2004.

wrongs done in His name. Yet, they do not apply the same principle to all the wrongs done in the name of atheism, nor address all the good that has likewise been done in God's name, which in fairness is not an argument for God any more than hypocrisy is a valid argument against God. The behavior of Christians neither confirms nor refutes the existence of God, just as the delayed flight has nothing to do with loaning out a lawnmower.

THE HYPOCRISY OF THE HYPOCRISY ARGUMENT

Those who want to use hypocrisy in the church by pointing to evils done as evidence against God in defense of atheism are being hypocritical. It is a straw man argument as the evil done in the name of atheism far exceeds anything done in the name of God or Jesus. This is not to excuse or to say that evil has not been done in the name of Christianity, but to recognize that the "wheat" and the "weeds" grow together. Teachings have been misinterpreted. At times Christians miss it. However, that is not a reflection on God, Jesus, or Christianity, but on the failures of people.

How many of you cherish it when someone points out everything that is wrong with you, but nothing right? Many argue against God by cherry-picking history, pointing out and exaggerating evils done while simultaneously neglecting how Christianity inspired justice, the abolition of slavery, third-world education, higher education in general, women's rights, serving the poorest of the poor, building hospitals, offering a response to national disasters, etc., all inspired by the teachings of Jesus.

For every negative that you can pull from the annals of history, there are countless positive examples of Christians living out their faith and making a positive impact on the culture at large, often at great cost to themselves. Once again, "We are never to judge a philosophy by its abuse."[9] Every negative can be countered by a greater good. Christianity has made great contributions to society. Still Christianity rises or falls on Jesus, not the successes or failures of the church. The real argument will not be found in how well or poorly the church has done, but in Who Jesus is.

WOLVES IN SHEEP'S CLOTHING

The world denounces hypocrisy. So did Jesus. Is it true that there are hypocrites in the church? Absolutely. Just as there are hypocrites in every institution and every field. However, hypocrites in the church doesn't make all Christians hypocrites nor is it a valid argument against the existence of God.

Consider, if I offered you a $20 bill, the real deal, government-issued, it would have the value of $20. What if I inserted that $20 bill into the midst of a pile of counterfeit $20s? Would you still want the government-issued $20 bill? Its value remains unchanged even if placed among counterfeit bills. "Wheat" and "weeds" grow together, but the presence of "weeds" does not diminish the value of the "wheat." The truth of Jesus' teachings remains unaffected by those who fail to live them out. People at times get focused on the "weeds" as an argument against God without considering the "wheat" and the argument that it may present for God (though, as I mentioned above and will point out below, both are ultimately irrelevant as God either exists or not independent of what people do or believe).

---

9   https://quotefancy.com/quote/905829/Saint-Augustine-Never-judge-a-philosophy-by-its-abuse.

Jesus warns, "Beware of false prophets, who come to you in sheep's clothing but inwardly are ravenous wolves."[10] People are not always what they seem; pretenders project an illusion—here described as wolves in sheep's clothing. Deceptive people rarely reveal their deception. They do not say, "I am only claiming to speak for God, but I am lying." Or "You do not want to listen to me as I am only using religion as a means to my ends, looking out for numero uno." This is the essence of hypocrisy—pretending to be someone or something you are not. Jesus continues:

> You will recognize them by their fruits. Are grapes gathered from thornbushes, or figs from thistles? [17] So, every healthy tree bears good fruit, but the diseased tree bears bad fruit. [18] A healthy tree cannot bear bad fruit, nor can a diseased tree bear good fruit. [19] Every tree that does not bear good fruit is cut down and thrown into the fire. [20] Thus you will recognize them by their fruits.[11]

This standard is both challenging and revealing. Some use it selectively to dismiss Christianity entirely— "Look at the Crusades! Look at televangelists exploiting the vulnerable!" Others use it selectively to celebrate Christianity's humanitarian achievements. The key point is that Jesus didn't just predict good fruit from His followers. He also anticipated corruption.

---

10 Matthew 7:15.
11 Matthew 7:16–20.

> Not everyone who says to me, 'Lord, Lord,' will enter the kingdom of heaven, but the one who does the will of my Father who is in heaven. [22] On that day many will say to me, 'Lord, Lord, did we not prophesy in your name, and cast out demons in your name, and do many mighty works in your name?' [23] And then will I declare to them, 'I never knew you; depart from me, you workers of lawlessness.'[12]

Jesus forewarned that people would *claim* His name while *contradicting* His teachings. He acknowledged the reality of hypocrisy before the first charge could be leveled against His followers. Ironically, criticizing Christianity for having hypocrites only confirms what Jesus predicted adding to His credibility.

THE NATURE OF HUMANITY

The presence of hypocrites, in the church or elsewhere, says nothing for or against the reality of God, it only exposes the nature of humanity. Keep in mind that the value of the fake is measured by how closely it can resemble that which is true. I did a mission trip to Cambodia in 2018 where I was surprised to find a $100 bill lying on the ground. Lucky me—not. It was counterfeit. Only, I didn't know, nor did anyone on our team, because we didn't know what to look for until our translator told us how to tell the difference. Counterfeits derive their value only in relation to something genuine. No one bothers to forge Monopoly money. Likewise, hypocrites in the church

---

12   Matthew 7:21–23.

do not disprove Christianity; rather, they highlight the value of the authentic faith they fail to represent.

But fruit inspectors beware and be aware that fruit takes time to ripen. It is important not to confuse hypocrisy with sin. Brokenness does not equate to hypocrisy. All Christians are still sinners, just like everyone else, but that doesn't make them a hypocrite. A hypocrite is pretending to be something or someone they are not, whereas a true Christian admits to being a sinner who is growing up over time in learning what it means to follow Jesus. I am not yet fully who I want to be, but neither am I who I once was. Transformation is a process that takes time. Just because I come to faith doesn't mean I am instantly and completely changed, but over time I should begin bearing more of the fruit of faith.

THE TRUTHFULNESS OF A CLAIM

Not everyone who claims to follow Jesus is following Jesus. However, just because someone lives inconsistently with a claim has no bearing on whether the claim is true or untrue. For instance, most people would claim that it is a good idea to live within their means, but that doesn't mean that they are. Or, that they would be better off if they exercised, that doesn't mean they will. The validity of the claim is independent of whether it is followed.

I have had periods in my life when I have been stricter with my diet and other seasons not quite so strict with how I ate. In one season of life, I was very intentional for a few months. If it came out of a box or had added sugar, I didn't eat it. Only real food with no ingredient list. During this time, I had a conversation with my brother whose response to healthy eating choices was, "I may die younger, but I'll die happier."

The truth or falsehood of a claim is not conditional on how well people do or do not follow it but on the claim itself. Will you benefit from living within your means, exercising regularly, and eating well? Most likely, if you are most people. You may have special exceptions that need to be considered but in general, these are true claims separately of whether they are followed. The question isn't whether Christ's followers have perfectly embodied His teachings (they haven't), but whether His teachings and claims are true.

FOLLOWING EVIDENCE

Hypocrisy is not an argument against God nor is good behavior an argument for God; herein is the fallacy of the hypocrisy argument. Either God exists or doesn't independent of how so-called Christians do or don't behave. Christian activities can be done by non-Christians just as there are Christians who can do unchristian things. The real question isn't what the church has or hasn't done, been or not been, whether there are or aren't hypocrites, but Who is Jesus? Christians will stumble and fall as Christianity is not a boxed meal where you just add water and presto, instant mature Christian. An immature believer may look hypocritical to the world when they haven't had time or opportunity to mature, or when you do not know from where they started or how far they have already come. You may even perchance run into atheists or people from other religions who appear more "Christlike" than some of the Christians you know. A claim is true or false independent of how well adherents follow or fail to follow it.

There will be pretenders in your midst, as well as Christians who occasionally simply miss the mark or mess up. That doesn't change whether God exists, the Bible is true, or

Jesus is real, which are entirely different issues than hypocrisy in the church, or many of the straw man arguments raised as excuses against God. For those questions, you must look to where the evidence leads and whether there is reason to believe based on the evidence.

If I were to cherry-pick the worst atheist to represent all atheists, the atheist would cry unfair; yet that is how hypocrisy has been used against God and Christianity rather than an honest evaluation of the evidence at hand. Leo Tolstoy wrote,

> Attack me, I do this myself, but attack me rather than the path I follow and which I point out to anyone who asks me where I think it lies. If I know the way home and am walking along it drunkenly, is it any less the right way because I am staggering from side to side![13]

My *staggering* doesn't change if it is the *right* way, it only reflects how well or poorly I walk in it.

For those of you who have children, would you say that your children reflect you and what you have taught them perfectly? Do they always make the decision you would make, behave as you would behave, do as you would do, and think as you would think? It is probably more likely the case, that you have at times said to a spouse, "Guess what your child did," or perhaps you made the comment, "We did not raise you that way," for they were acting contrary to what they were taught. That doesn't diminish what they were taught, it only establishes that they didn't perfectly keep it.

---

13   Clark, Mark. *The Problem of God: Answering a Skeptic's Challenges to Christianity*. Grand Rapids, Michigan: Zondervan, 2017, p185.

Christians, even well-intentioned ones, act contrary to the teachings of Jesus at times. However, that is not a reflection on the teachings of Jesus or the reality of God, but a reflection on us. The premise of the gospel is not what you can do for God, but what God has done for you. The world looks at the church and says, "There are broken people there, God can't be real." However, I am in the church because I recognize that I am broken and need God. The world fails to see that it was precisely because people were broken that Jesus came to put the pieces back together. The truth of God and Christianity doesn't rise or fall on the morality, or lack thereof, of Christians, but the reality of Jesus. For that, you must look at the best explanations for the evidence and whether it supports faith in God, specifically the God made known in and through Jesus.

If hypocrisy is not a valid argument against God, are there valid arguments for God? One of the things I like to share with people at church is that faith is not a blind leap but a reasonable step. You may not have all the answers, but God has given you enough reason to believe and take the step of faith. Will you take this journey with me to see if faith in God and following Jesus is a reasonable step for you? If so, let's read on.

Chapter 2

Faith is a Reasonable Step, not a Blind Leap

Romans 1:18-23

Do you have reason to believe in the reality of God beyond simply taking a "blind leap" of faith, as some may say? Is belief in God reasonable? Of course, saying that faith is a reasonable step requires more than simply pointing out that many arguments against God are straw man arguments. As we concluded in the last chapter, if hypocrisy is not a valid line of defense against God, are there compelling grounds for God's existence?

PERSONAL TESTIMONY

I've had an experience that I'm guessing isn't unique to me, and it's probably one that almost everyone has had at one point or another: making an order from Amazon.com. Anyone else guilty? So, if you're like me and you've ordered from Amazon. com, one of the things that you've probably had happen is before you even get your item to test out, you've had something land in your e-mail box saying, "Please review your product." I refuse to review anything that I do not have personal experience with yet. And, honestly, most of the time, I don't have a whole lot to say even after receiving it. You know, when it comes to Braun cleaning fluid there isn't much to review. Reviews on some products seem pointless as it either works or it doesn't.

Nonetheless, there are items that you are likely to read a review before making a purchase, as you would like to know what others have to say. So, you go to the reviews and inevitably there are five-star and one-star reviews, most helpful and least helpful. Just for fun, I went to Amazon.com and there was a big banner at the top advertising the Echo dot, and I thought, "why not?" Let's see what the reviews say.

There were five-star reviews as well as one-star reviews, so I thought I would explore the extremes. When I went to read the one-star review the assessment was that it needed more security. The Bluetooth on the Echo Dot was connecting with someone's Bluetooth on his cell phone. Nothing like listening to people's cell phone calls on your Echo Dot as they drive by. I guess if you are driving down the street by people's homes you may want to turn off that Bluetooth, as who knows who may be listening in. To be fair, I randomly chose a review and selected a negative one. The Echo Dot had far more positive reviews than negative ones.

But there's another name for reviews—one that sounds a little bit more, shall we say, Christianese: testimonials. Who doesn't love a good testimony? Last Friday I went to visit a couple who had visited our church. We had some coffee and bread as we sat down at the kitchen table to visit, and they said, "Well, we might as well get the good news and the bad news out front." I'm like, "OK." Straight to the point. Hoping as all do that the good comments will outweigh the bad.

They had written their "review" on a sticky note. On one side they had written all the good things they had to say. "Warm welcome. Friendly people. Chairs, A++. Holy Spirit. Bible Based. Great music. Great message. The sermon notes are excellent. Organized. Tables like home. Instantly felt like family." On the other side what we needed to improve on. It was blank. Now that's a testimony I could get used to. I enjoyed the visit, and the coffee and bread were good too.

Personal testimonies are much like product reviews, whether about one's experience at church or more significantly, "This is what God has done for me." However, there will be those who counter that God is only a figment of the imagination, a fabrication that evolved for our survival or coping, wishful thinking, or a crutch for the weak. That we invent a world of make-believe to avoid the harshness of the real world. However, who is living in the world of make-believe? Certainly, there are people with a strong desire to believe in God, that there is something more to life; it is likewise true that there are those with a strong desire to not believe in God because they dislike the idea that they may be accountable for how they live. What I *desire* or *dislike* doesn't determine what is true, so which is inventing a world of make-believe?

EVEN SCIENCE RELIES ON FAITH

As nice as testimonies are, you cannot rely only on experience as that only invites the response, "What you believe works for you, but this works for me." Part of the problem of today's age is people want to relativize absolutes and make absolutes relative. Who hasn't heard someone claim, "There is no such thing as absolute truth." You do realize that is an absolute statement that thereby contradicts itself. God either exists, or

God doesn't, and it has nothing to do with what I may or may not desire. The critical question is not what do I wish to be true, but what do I have reason to believe is true?

Atheism wants to take away a cause for the universe, seeming to imply "Why couldn't it just be?" Hmm? Why couldn't you get something (the universe) from nothing (science says the universe had a beginning)? That doesn't sound very scientific to me. They want to strip away a Designer from what appears to be impressively designed, and as many scientists exclaim, "fine-tuned" for life. In addition to how it all got started, absent God you are hard pressed to find, or create, a basis for how the nonliving transitioned to living and nonconscious moved to consciousness—these are unsolved problems in science.

Christians highlight that the existence of a design in the intricacies of creation is best explained by the reality of a Designer. The slightest deviations in any number of variables would make life impossible. William Paley is attributed with the analogy of the watch and the watchmaker. If you are walking along a beach and stumble upon a watch your assumption will not be that it was assembled over time, but that someone had assembled it. The presence of design is an indicator for a Designer.[14] How much more complex is human DNA than that of a watch? The complexity of DNA suggests an intelligent Creator behind it.[15]

The scientific "Big Bang" theory teaches us that the universe had a beginning, which begs the question, "What, or Who caused it to begin?" I was listening to a Joe Rogan

---

14   Paley, William Paley. *Natural Theology*, New York: E. Sargeant and Company,1802.

15   *The Language of God: A Scientist Presents Evidence for Belief* by Francis Collins.

interview with Wesley Huff where Rogan quoted Terence McKenna, whose name I missed, but commented, "Even science requires one miracle."[16] Science cannot answer how life started. "As Allan Rex Sandage, said to be the greatest observational cosmologist of all time, has said: 'It is my science that drove me to the conclusion that the world is much more complicated than can be explained by science.'"[17] From the origin of the universe and its fine-tuning for life to the concept of 'irreducible complexity' in biology and the existence of consciousness and morality, numerous scientific and philosophical arguments are best explained by the reality of God. Likewise, where does your inherent sense of right and wrong come from? Why does a moral law transcend cultures when strict evolutionary theory suggests only a 'survival of the fittest' mentality? Christians argue that we have a moral law because there is a moral Lawgiver.

You may be disappointed to hear me say that from a scientific perspective, God can neither be proved nor disproved. Science, by definition, is a branch of knowledge or study dealing with facts or truths gained through observation and experimentation. Despite our desires to put our faith in science, science has limitations. As the Bible makes clear— and as Godel's incompleteness theorem and Heisenberg's uncertainty principle affirm—logic isn't powerful enough to make sense of the real world. Intuition and faith pick up where logic and scientific experiments leave off.[18] It isn't always what evidence can prove, but sometimes it is what best explains the evidence you have.

16 "The Joe Rogan Experience," episode #2252.
17 Clark, Mark. *The Problem of God: Answering a Skeptic's Challenges to Christianity.* Grand Rapids, Michigan: Zondervan, 2017, p.38.
18 Guillen, Dr. Michael. *Amazing Truths: How Science and the Bible Agree.* Grand Rapids, Michigan: Zondervan, 2015, p.110.

Whether in the name of science, or the name of religion, at some point, everyone is relying on faith or philosophical perspectives to answer questions that go beyond science. Despite false accusations that have occasionally been made, the Bible and science are not in conflict but complementary. Throughout history, great scientists have believed in God, many of whom became scientists believing that by studying creation they would better know its Creator.

TRUTH EXPRESSED OR TRUTH SUPPRESSED?

Romans 1:18-32 is not what you would call one of the more glamorous passages of Scripture, as it confronts you with a hard truth: the tendency to suppress the truth you do not like. What truth is being suppressed? Romans 1:18-20 tells us,

> [18] For the wrath of God is revealed from heaven against all ungodliness and unrighteousness of men, who by their unrighteousness suppress the truth. [19] For what can be known about God is plain to them, because God has shown it to them. [20] For his invisible attributes, namely, his eternal power and divine nature, have been clearly perceived, ever since the creation of the world, in the things that have been made. So they are without excuse.[19]

The truth being suppressed is the reality of God as revealed through creation. There you have it. The Bible says so, case closed. Except, I have not dealt with the uniqueness and

---

19   Romans 1:18–20.

trustworthiness of the Bible yet (chapter 3), so I must explore other reasons to believe that are outside the Bible itself.

As it turns out, the problem is not the absence of evidence, but the suppression of truth, or the best explanation for the evidence we have. Now wait a minute, science doesn't suppress the truth, but pursues it... Does it? If the Covid pandemic of 2020 taught us anything it was that science can be politically hijacked and is sometimes manipulated for reasons other than pure science.[20] Throughout the duration of the pandemic, I listened to doctors and scientists who were censored by mainline media and attacked by other doctors and scientists because they exposed the truth that was not politically expedient. Fortunately, their voices were eventually vindicated as the truth slowly emerged and exposed the cover up done in the name of science.

Astronomer Sir Arther Eddington said, "Philosophically the notion of a beginning of the present order of nature is repugnant to me.... I should like to find a genuine loophole."[21] As I researched this topic, I was shocked by the number of scientists who essentially said, "...it doesn't matter whether a scientific theory is correct or not, as long as it gets rid of the need for the supernatural." Did you know that scientists originally rejected the Big Bang theory because it gave too much credibility to, "in the beginning God created..." (Gen. 1:1)? Inescapably, it was shown that the universe is expanding, thank you Hubble telescope, disclosing that the universe was

20   Ruse, Austin. *Fake Science: Exposing the Left's skewed statistics, fuzzy facts, and dodgy data*. Washington D.C.: Regnery Publishing, 2017. This book was written before 2020; however, it elaborates several examples of how science has been hijacked to serve political ends.

21   Eddington, Sir Arther. 1931. "The End of the World: From the Standpoint of Mathematical Physics." *Nature*, vol. 127, p. 450.

not self-existent; it had a point of origin in which it began, the Big Bang!

"There is an old adage, 'It is better to debate a question [in this case the existence of God] before settling it than to settle a question before debating it.'"[22] Noted atheist Bertrand Russell was asked, "If you meet God after you die, what will you say to Him to justify your unbelief? 'I will tell Him that He did not give me enough evidence.'"[23] Paul tells you in Romans 1 that the debate doesn't center on the evidence but on the interpretation of the evidence. God's eternal power and divine nature are seen throughout creation leaving you without excuse.

Have you ever quipped, "I should have seen the writing on the wall; the clues were all there—I just didn't pay attention"? We are amazingly gifted at not seeing what we would rather not be true. The Message paraphrases Romans 1:20, "By taking a long and thoughtful look at what God has created, people have always been able to see what their eyes as such can't see: eternal power, for instance, and the mystery of his divine being. So nobody has a good excuse."[24] Alister McGrath highlights eight clues in *Mere Apologetics*, pointing out that the power of the clues is in the cumulative effect of all the clues combined. You can also check out, *Evidence for God: 50 Arguments for Faith from the Bible, History, Philosophy, and Science*, if you want to explore the arguments more deeply.

---

22   Zacharias, Ravi. *Jesus Among Other Gods: The Absolute Claims of the Christian Message*. Nashville, Tennessee: Word Publishing, 2000, p47. After Ravi's death, a scandal broke out regarding his character. While I do not condone any moral failings, it doesn't change the truth of what he said.

23   Ibid., p47.

24   Peterson, E. H. (2005). *The Message: the Bible in contemporary language* (Ro 1:20). NavPress.

For the sake of space, I will not unload fifty arguments on you but stick with creation since it pertains to the Romans 1 text.

WHISPERS IN THE COSMOS

The first reason to believe in the reality of God is simply that you exist. Science explains volumes about life, though many facts continue to elude science, such as why there is "something" rather than "nothing." I propose that faith in God is more reasonable than faith in something coming from nothing, and life coming from nonlife. Creation is a billboard publicizing the glory of God. In Luke 19 Jesus makes His triumphal entry into Jerusalem and some of the Pharisees asked Jesus to rebuke His disciples for their praise. "[Jesus] answered, 'I tell you, if these were silent, the very stones would cry out.'" [25] Romans 1 concurs. The stones are crying out as creation testifies to its Creator. "The heavens declare the glory of God, and the sky above proclaims his handiwork."[26]

The looming question is why is there something rather than nothing; how did life emerge from nonlife? For something to begin depends on a cause that preexisted it. It used to be believed that the preexistent something was the universe itself until Edwin Hubble proved otherwise. The Bible and the Big Bang are not in conflict, but complementary. God spoke and "Bang," as some like to say. Before the "Big Bang Theory" became a popular TV show as the reigning scientific theory, it had been rejected by scientists because if the universe didn't always exist, that meant it had a beginning, a point of origin, raising the question of how the universe

---

25   Luke 19:40.
26   Psalm 19:1.

came to be.[27] Amazing as it is, the universe could not create itself. "The award-winning scientist who mapped the human genome, Francis Collins agrees: 'The Big Bang cries out for a divine explanation…It forces the conclusion that nature had a defined beginning. I cannot see how nature could have created itself. Only a supernatural force that is outside of space and time could have done that.'"[28]

EXPLOSIVE ORDER

Count the natural disasters that led to order rather than disorder. Didn't take long, did it? How many explosions spawn structure in their aftermath rather than creating chaos? In other words, how many explosions are needed before something beautiful is created or until life emerges? Science cannot explain why there is something rather than nothing, it cannot explain how the biggest bang in all of history resulted in a system finely tuned and designed for life. Science depends on the order and structure of the universe yet can't explain why it is there. Beyond debate is that everything appears designed for life. Your concern is the interpretation of how and why, whether it is best explained by time and chance or by the existence of God.

In his writings and radio commentaries, Chuck Colson talks about the anthropic principle: the structure of the universe is exactly what is needed to support life. The distance to the sun, the strength of gravity, that water expands and floats when it freezes (unlike most substances), the electrical forces in electrons, etc. "The anthropic principle makes a

---

27   Guillen, Dr. Michael. *Amazing Truths: How Science and the Bible Agree.* Grand Rapids, Michigan: Zondervan, 2015, chapter 6.
28   Clark, Mark. *The Problem of God: Answering a Skeptic's Challenges to Christianity.* Grand Rapids, Michigan: Zondervan, 2017, p56.

chance creation so improbable as to be absurd."[29] It takes more faith to believe that a random explosion (that occurred when there was nothing and without any explanation) "created" a universe with such order and structure as to be perfectly designed for life.

> The mathematical chances of our universe ever coming into existence are so tiny that they are at the level of the miraculous. But that's not all. The chances that all the life-permitting variables needed to line up perfectly to birth our universe within such a specific range are so low that mathematicians tell us they cry out for an explanation. The improbability of the existence of our universe begs us to wonder how it exists at all. Scholars tell us that the chance of our universe coming into existence is one chance in 10^{138} …. Astrophysicists tell us that there were around 122 variables that would have had to be lined up in precise values in order for our universe to come into existence, and if any of those was off by even one part in a million millionth '[m]atter would not have been able to coalesce. There would have been no galaxies, no stars, no plants, and no people.'[30]

Princeton physicist Freeman Dyson is well known for this quote, "The more I examine the universe and the details of its architecture, the more evidence I find that the universe in some

29   Colson, Chuck. https://breakpoint.org/more-than-coincidence/
30   Clark, Mark. *The Problem of God: Answering a Skeptic's Challenges to Christianity.* Grand Rapids, Michigan: Zondervan, 2017, p57-58.

sense must have known we were coming."[31] How do you get an intelligent design, with intricate order, precise measurements of gravity, distances, rotations, oxygen, carbon dioxide, nitrogen, planets, stars, etc., all perfectly suited to start and support life? A random explosion (with nothing to explode?) plus random chance over time, or an Intelligence like God? Which requires more faith?[32]

While the Bible is not a science book, it is reconcilable with science, and many scientists have believed in God, just as many have rejected the idea of God. Richard Dawkins proposes a multiverse where there may be trillions of universes and so it is inevitable that one would sustain life. Perhaps you have noticed that Hollywood has even picked up this multiverse theme in some of its movies. However, there is no evidence for a multiverse, and, even if you concede a multiverse, you are still left with the impasse: how did it begin?

Not only Is there order required for life, but what of morality, consciousness, desire, beauty, and relationality? Alvin Plantinga, considered by many to be one of the greatest philosophers of modern times, points out that two dozen philosophical arguments for God's existence reveal it is more rational to believe God exists than not to. "[Plantinga] argues for the existence of God at such a high and convincing level that Smith says, 'In philosophy, it became, almost overnight, 'academically respectable' to argue for theism.'"[33]

---

31   https://www.goodreads.com/quotes/309377.

32   If you want to explore which takes greater faith more, check out Geisler, Norman and Turek, Frank. *I Don't Have Enough Faith to Be an Atheist, (Crossway, 2004).*

33   Clark, Mark. *The Problem of God: Answering a Skeptic's Challenges to Christianity.* Grand Rapids, Michigan: Zondervan, 2017, p25.

> For although they knew God, they did not
> honor him as God or give thanks to him, but they
> became futile in their thinking, and their foolish
> hearts were darkened. [22] Claiming to be wise,
> they became fools, [23] and exchanged the glory of
> the immortal God for images resembling mortal
> man and birds and animals and creeping things.[34]

Claiming to be wise, they became fools. Another translation says their thinking became nonsense. With the evidence before us people have declared that somehow, we got something out of nothing, life defied all science by emerging from nonlife, we are part of a multiverse, or, if you watch the History Channel, perhaps we were planted here by alien intelligence. These are all theories with no scientific proof; vain attempts to eliminate any semblance of the supernatural. A speck of infinite density called a singularity for an unknown reason exploded. Contrary to any other explosion ever observed anytime and anywhere, this one led to order, design, and beauty, along with the sophisticated system with exact precision required for life. Some explain the beauty and complexity you see as nothing more than emerging from an explosion, others from a Creator. Which explanation requires more "blind faith"? Which offers a more "reasonable step"?

Romans 1:23 likely refers to Israel's bowing down before the golden calf. Today, we are too sophisticated for that. Our culture's "golden calf" is evolution as the glory of God has been exchanged for the process of natural selection. However, evolution has no satisfactory answers as to how it all began. Astronomer Robert Jastrow wrote, "For the scientist who has

---

34 Romans 1:21–23.

lived by his faith in the power of reason, the story ends like a bad dream. He has scaled the mountains of ignorance; he is about to conquer the highest peak; as he pulls himself over the final rock, he is greeted by a band of theologians who have been sitting there for centuries."[35]

"In the beginning, God created" (Gen. 1:1). When you examine the world around you, it is more reasonable to believe in God than to not believe. "For what can be known about God is plain to them, because God has shown it to them. [20] For his invisible attributes, namely, his eternal power and divine nature, have been clearly perceived, ever since the creation of the world, in the things that have been made. So they are without excuse."[36] Faith explains the order, design, and structure that science depends on to work.

> The Christian has a worldview based on the belief that God exists. The atheist has a worldview based on that belief that God doesn't. The Christian cannot prove that God exists, but the atheist cannot prove that God doesn't. Both worldviews are based on faith. The question is, which worldview has the strongest evidence to support the faith of its adherents?[37]

The reality of God cannot scientifically be proven or disproven, but if you read the reviews or testimonials of the universe, they point you to a Creator. Faith is not a blind leap—it is a reasonable response to the testimony of creation, the best explanation for the evidence. The impending question

---

35   Jastrow, Robert. *God and the Astronomers,* (Second edition, 1992), p116.

36   Romans 1:19–20.

37   Merritt, James. *God, I've Got a Question: Biblical Truth for Our Deepest Concerns.* Eugene, Oregon: Harvest House, 2011, p21-22.

is how will you respond to the evidence that God has given? For those who don't believe, I invite you to truly examine what is the most reasonable explanation for what you see around you. God is big enough for honest scrutiny and there are many arguments for the reality of God that are beyond the scope of this book. For those who do believe, I pray that you may be better equipped to engage the doubts of the world around you and that you are encouraged to live in a way that gives God the glory due to His name.

Of course, the lingering question is, if you have reason to believe in the reality of God, how do you come to know Him personally? You can only know someone to the degree that they make themselves known, so how has God chosen to reveal Himself beyond what creation declares?

Chapter 3

A Book Like No Other, The Trustworthiness of the Bible

2 Timothy 3:10-17

*You can only know someone to the degree
that they make themselves known. How has
God chosen to reveal Himself? What sets
the Bible apart from any other book?*

Not only is less faith required to believe in God than to not believe, but you also have ample basis for accepting His revelation through the Bible. No other book has undergone more inspection, and criticism, yet rises above scrutiny to reveal itself as trustworthy and true, remaining relevant for all time as a means of God's self-revelation to you.

NOT A BUFFET

Many of you enjoy eating out. My wife, Amanda, believes that everything tastes better if you don't have to cook it. I prefer home-cooked, but since I am not the one doing the home-cooking, I can't complain. That said, I enjoy a good buffet from time to time—eat what you like, leave what you don't, and never walk away hungry. Miserable, maybe, but not hungry. I can't tell you how many times we have paid too much for a meal only for me to leave hungry—and that doesn't make Dan happy. But leaving hungry has never happened with a buffet.

When it comes to the Bible, people tend to take one of two approaches. Some discount it all together and leave it off their plate, thinking of it as rubbish, myth, fake, or outdated. Others treat it like a buffet, picking and choosing what they like while ignoring what they dislike. They pile on all the messages of love, grace, mercy, compassion, and faithfulness while turning their noses up at passages about sin, falling short, and judgment. *I'll have a double helping of God's love—hold the holiness, please.*

I had a professor at seminary who taught, "There are times we must preach against the biblical text." He reasoned that there is a canon within the canon of Scripture which is God's love. If the term canon is unfamiliar to you, think of a "measuring stick," or a standard or rule by which spiritual truth is measured. If a passage seemed to contradict or deny God's love he argued, "You must preach against it."

This naturally raised some questions for me, such as, *how do you know that God loves you in the first place?* This professor, like many others, would point to the fact that God sent His Son, Jesus, to die for you on the cross. But how do you know that? *The Bible.* How do you know that Jesus' death was an act of love rather than just a case of angering the wrong people? *The Bible.* How do you know that His death was sacrificial and meant for the forgiveness of sins? *The Bible.* How do you define what love is and what love looks like? *The Bible.*

Sources outside the Bible confirm Jesus' existence, His crucifixion, and that His followers believed in His resurrection. However, the Bible reveals the motivations and meaning behind these events. What if I argued that Jesus' death on the cross for the forgiveness of my sins was a denial of God's love for Jesus—therefore, something I should preach against? That would be nonsense, as His death is the central expression of how God has demonstrated His love for you.[38]

You cannot approach the Scriptures as a buffet line where you can pick and choose what you like and dislike, what to believe or disbelieve. If you do, you lose the foundation for the whole. You make yourself the arbiter of truth. You must wrestle with whether the Bible is man's words about God or God's words to man. Paul writes,

> All Scripture is breathed out by God and profitable for teaching, for reproof, for correction, and for training in righteousness, [17] that the man of God may be complete, equipped for every good work.[39]

You have reason to believe in the reality of God. Do you likewise have reason to trust the reliability of Scripture—that it is God's word to you?

NOT JUST ANOTHER BOOK

It is no secret that many doubt the legitimacy of the Bible. Some have accused the Bible of being out of date, irrelevant,

---

38   Romans 5:1-11.
39   2 Timothy 3:16–17.

sexist, boring, and a waste of time. Some characterize it as a book of myths filled with contradictions. Others may concede that it is a good book with moral lessons but not the word of God—perhaps inspiring in parts while objectionable in other parts.

In the last chapter, we explored some evidence highlighting the rationality of believing in God. This begs the question: how do you know this God? Is He distant or personal? Can you have a relationship with God, and if so, how? These questions are addressed in the Bible; nonetheless, before you turn to the Bible for answers you must ask, "Can I trust the Bible?" Numerous religious books exist, all claiming their legitimacy, yet not all hold up under scrutiny. Just as you have a basis to believe God is real, there are reasons to trust that God has revealed Himself through the Bible.

"But as for you, continue in what you have learned and have firmly believed, knowing from whom you learned it".[40] Paul exhorts Timothy to continue in what he had learned. This comes right after warning him against imposters deceiving and being deceived (2 Timothy 3:13), as well as being real with the need for "reproof" and "correction" (3:16). Learning is like the weather—it changes. Some things you believe to be true today may be proven false tomorrow. Other things you may think false may be proven true. Anyone who has attempted to eat healthily knows this all too well as the "experts" appear to change their minds on what healthy eating looks like, and which diet is the best to follow. Science operates on the premise of a hypothesis—thought to be true and worth bearing investigation—but at times, that investigation requires rethinking the original hypothesis. When Paul writes to

---

40   2 Timothy 3:14.

Timothy about what he has "learned and firmly believed", the Greek means that which he has been persuaded by and is sure of the trustworthiness and validity of. It wasn't simply that Timothy learned it, but that Timothy found it to be true. He was convinced.

"No other written work has been so attacked, scrutinized, and persecuted as have the canonical books of the Bible. ... [yet] the Bible has withstood all forms of oppression."[41] Incidentally, Josh McDowell has over 100 pages speaking to the uniqueness of the Bible which I do not intend to duplicate. This is one chapter in a book aiming to establish reason for trusting the Bible in what it says about Jesus, not a book focused solely on the trustworthiness of the Bible. If you need more investigation than I offer here, please refer to works by Josh McDowell, Erwin Lutzer, James Merritt, and Timothy Keller, or others who dig into this topic more deeply. I intend to share thoughts that are not unique to me but provide a concise summary of why you can trust the Bible so that I can utilize it as a source for establishing the uniqueness of Jesus without falling prey to circular reasoning. The Bible holds up under scrutiny, so I have no fear in inviting and encouraging you to investigate it further if you need to.

THE ENDURING MESSAGE

If you open a Bible in your hand, or your smartphone, there will inevitably be a printing date. Your current printing was not the first, and certainly not the original document, nor

---

41   McDowell, Josh & Sean. *Evidence that Demands a Verdict: A Life Changing Truth For A Skeptical World.* Nashville, Tennessee: Thomas Nelson, 2017, p3-139. I highly recommend this resource if you would like to do a deep dive into the evidence for the uniqueness of the Bible, the uniqueness of Jesus, and the knowability of truth as it covers a wide range of topics in great depth.

even the original language of Hebrew, Aramaic, or Greek, which raises the question of how do you know if your copy accurately represents the originals. Critics are quick to point out the "telephone game" where if I whisper a message to one person, and he or she to another, and so on around the room, the message will have changed by the time it gets back to me. The more times the message is transmitted the more it will be altered.

Paul writes, "I am reminded of your sincere faith, a faith that dwelt first in your grandmother Lois and your mother Eunice and now, I am sure, dwells in you as well",[42] and he encourages Timothy to "continue in what he has learned".[43] How do you know that what Timothy learned was the same as what his mother and grandmother learned? Is it possible to pass along information without it getting corrupted in transmission? Let's try this little exercise. For most of you, if I start a slogan, you can complete it before I do, despite many years since its inception.

- "Just … do it" (Nike, 1988).
- "Where's the … beef" (Wendy's, 1984).
- "Melts in your mouth, not in your … hands" (M&M's, 1967).
- "Gimme a break, gimme a break, give me a piece of that … Kit Kat Bar" (Kit Kat, 1957).

As many times as the Bible has been copied throughout history, how do you know that you are learning the same thing that Timothy learned?

---

42   2 Timothy 1:5.
43   2 Timothy 3:14.

Keep in mind that I am not addressing interpretations of the text, but the source material, the text itself. We suffer today from thinking everything is about us, and we measure others by our experience. If we struggle with attention deficit, then why should we expect, they could focus any better? Quite frankly, they are not us. They did not grow up with television, commercials, and rapid-fire sound bites, with information readily at their fingertips; all of which has retrained our brains to not focus on retaining information since it is easily retrievable elsewhere. Their culture was not only trained in passing along oral traditions, but they meticulously preserved the Scriptures, believing them inspired by God.

In their copying, they counted lines, they counted words, they counted letters, and then they recounted with independent sources. They checked, double-checked, and triple-checked their copies. It has been said that up to two errors could be corrected, but three required starting over. They painstakingly sought to preserve the originals through the copies for the copies were then to carry the authority of the originals. With that said, intent doesn't always carry over into practice. Despite my intent as a preacher, sometimes I fumble over words. How can you be assured that we have "good copies?"

The reliability of a historical text is determined by the number of manuscripts available, the time interval between the date of events and the date of writing, and the quality of the manuscripts. No other accepted historical work compares to the Bible in our ability to verify its accuracy in keeping true to the original as illustrated in this chart.

AUTHOR	BOOK	DATE WRITTEN	EARLIEST COPIES	TIME GAP	NO. OF COPIES
Homer	Iliad	800 B.C.	c. 400 B.C.	c. 400 yrs.	643
Herodotus	History	480–425 B.C.	c. A.D. 900	c. 1,350 yrs.	8
Thucydides	History	460–400 B.C.	c. A.D. 900	c. 1,300 yrs.	8
Plato		400 B.C.	c. A.D. 900	c. 1,300 yrs.	7
Demosthenes		300 B.C.	c. A.D. 1100	c. 1,400 yrs.	200
Caesar	Gallic Wars	100–44 B.C.	c. A.D. 900	c. 1,000 yrs.	10
Livy	History of Rome	59 B.C.–A.D. 17	4th cent. (partial) mostly 10th cent.	c. 400 yrs. c. 1,000 yrs.	1 partial 19 copies
Tacitus	Annals	A.D. 100	c. A.D. 1100	c. 1,000 yrs.	20
Pliny Secundus	Natural History	A.D. 61–113	c. A.D. 850	c. 750 yrs.	7
New Testament		A.D. 50–100	c. 114 (fragment) c. 200 (books) c. 250 (most of N.T.) c. 325 (complete N.T.)	+50 yrs. 100 yrs. 150 yrs. 225 yrs.	5366

[44]

Josh McDowell observes that if we stacked all the manuscripts we have to verify the Bible, it would rise 2.5 miles high.[45] That is impressive mileage, providing high assurance for accuracy.

In addition, our evidence is not limited to the New Testament; confirmation for the Old Testament came through the Dead Sea Scrolls. The discovery of the Dead Sea Scrolls was truly a godsend. The value of this discovery cannot be overstated as it provided manuscripts that predated what we had by one thousand years. The Dead Sea Scrolls confirmed that incredible accuracy was maintained in the copies. The

---

44   McDowell, J. (2006). _Evidence for Christianity_ (p. 315). Thomas Nelson Publishers. Used by permission. The evidence for the reliability of the New Testament has only increased since the time this chart was created, and more copies have been discovered. However, this chart still illustrates that the Bible is in a league of its own.

45   McDowell, Josh & Sean. _Evidence that Demands a Verdict: A Life Changing Truth for A Skeptical World._ Nashville, Tennessee: Thomas Nelson, 2017, p53.

only variations were slight and generally pertained to spelling differences, with no doctrinal differences. "No other book from the ancient world has as much manuscript support or is as closely tied to the original event as the Bible", [46] enabling us to construct 99.5% of the original document. No other historical work can make that claim.[47] We have better textual attestation to the New Testament than any other piece of ancient literature, making the Bible the most authenticated book in history.

SUPPORT FROM ARCHAEOLOGY AND SCIENCE

We can confidently say that our copies accurately reflect the originals. However, that does not close the case. In 2001, when I did a Clinical Pastoral Education unit, I was asked, "Is it more important to you to be right or to be understood?" I answered, "To be right; otherwise, what difference does it make if you understand me?" Who cares if the copies reflect the originals if the originals are not true? A lie repeated often enough may become believed as true, but that doesn't make it

46   Merritt, James. *God, I've Got a Question: Biblical Truth for Our Deepest Concerns.* Eugene, Oregon: Harvest House, 2011, p29.

47   "Some have challenged the accuracy of the New Testament (NT) manuscripts based on a statement in our book *A General Introduction to the Bible* that inadvertently attributed to Bruce Metzer the figure that the NT is copied with 99.5 percent accuracy. However, this is an inconsequential criticism for several reasons. First, NT textual authorities Westcott and Hort estimated that only about one-sixtieth rise above "trivialities" and can be called "substantial variations." In short, the NT is 98.33 percent pure. Second, Greek expert Ezra Abbott said about 19/20 (95 percent) of the readings are "various" rather than "rival" readings, and about 19/20 (95 percent) of the rest make no appreciable difference in the sense of the passage. Thus the text is 99.75 percent accurate. Third, noted NT Greek scholar A. T. Robertson said the real concern is with about a "thousandth part of the entire text." So, the reconstructed text of the New Testament is 99.9% free from real concern" (https://normangeisler.com/a-note-on-the-percent-of-accuracy-of-the-new-testament-text/).

true, or useful. Even if the copies reflect the originals, do you have reason to believe the originals themselves are trustworthy?

When I was in seminary, one of the classes that I took was "Introduction to the Old Testament." One day, our professor was absent. Rather than canceling class, she had her assistant show us a video of an archeologist who claimed that King David was a myth. He confidently boasted, "We know David was a myth because a man of that stature would have left a footprint. We haven't found this footprint so he must have been made up." It just so happened that as I commuted to seminary that week I was listening to a radio news show reporting about the archaeological discoveries proving the existence of King David. The problem was that we were watching a late-1980s video made before the discoveries.

I mentioned in class that since the time of the video archeologists had uncovered evidence for King David. Imagine my disbelief in learning that the teacher's assistant already knew this fact and showed the video anyway. We were watching a video that even our "teacher" knew to be patently false, overturned by new learning: new learning verifying the Bible's historical account. We were listening to an "expert" say the Bible got it wrong, while archeology proved the Bible was right. Repeatedly, people have questioned the history recorded in the Bible: The Hittites never existed, the walls of Jericho did not fall as recorded, King David was a myth, and Moses couldn't have written the first five books as writing hadn't been invented yet. All these claims were made with great confidence, yet in time they were all proven wrong. These allegations were disproven with new archaeological discoveries. Learning evolves, and, as it turns out, the more we learn only confirms what the Bible recorded.

Joseph Free, in *Archaeology and Bible History*, addresses the question of archaeology and its relationship to the Bible: We pointed out that numerous passages of the Bible which long puzzled the commentators have readily yielded up their meaning when new light from archaeological discoveries has been focused on them. In other words, archaeology illuminates the text of the Scriptures and so makes valuable contributions to the fields of biblical interpretation and exegesis. In addition to illuminating the Bible, archaeology has confirmed countless passages which have been rejected by critics as unhistorical or contradictory to known facts. (Free, ABH, 1)[48]

If "exegesis" is a new term for you, it means critical explanation or interpretation of a text. Dr. Clifford Wilson wrote, "I ... remember one of the world's leading archeologists at Gezer rebuking a younger archeologist who was 'rubbishing the Bible.' When the younger archeologist asked 'Why?', he replied, 'Well, it just has a habit of proving to be right after all.'"[49]

This is not to say that every historical detail in the Bible has been proven, however, when your track record is excellent you should be extended the benefit rather than the doubt. The Bible speaks extensively of that which can be and has

---

48   McDowell, J. (2006). *Evidence for Christianity* (p. 133). Thomas Nelson Publishers. While I have several quotes from this book, it is currently out of print. If you want to dive in deeper McDowell's *Evidence that Demands a Verdict (2017)* is a great apologetic resource.
49   Archaeologist confirms creation and the Bible: Interview with archaeologist Dr Clifford Wilson ... by Dr Carl Wieland, *Creation* 14(4):46–50, 1992; creation.com/clifford-wilson.

been verified historically. Biblical authors readily refer to names, places, events and numerous details that provide opportunities for investigation and under examination have been proven true. "Dr. Nelson Glueck, by consensus the greatest modern authority on Israeli archeology, said, 'No archeological discovery has ever controverted a biblical reference…archeology continues to confirm a clear outline or in exact detail historical statements in the Bible.'"[50] Archeology continues to confirm, sounds like archeology is playing catch up to the Bible.

Nonetheless, it isn't just archaeology. While the Bible is not a science book, it contains many scientific principles that were ahead of their time. For example, the Bible provides information about the earth being a sphere, the importance of blood for life and healing, how to handle contagious diseases, the stars being innumerable—concepts that contradicted the prevailing beliefs of the time (such as the flat earth theory, bloodletting, the need for washing and quarantining, and the number of stars)—but were later proven to be scientifically accurate. While the Bible is not a science book, it offers scientific insights that predated their acceptance in the scientific community.[51]

But what about the contradictions? Who hasn't heard that one before? The Bible is filled with contradictions as it says this here and that there. But what exactly constitutes a contradiction? One day I was out running, and I thought, "I could go home and say the skies were blue, or that it was partly

---

50   Merritt, James. *God, I've Got a Question: Biblical Truth for Our Deepest Concerns.* Eugene, Oregon: Harvest House, 2011, p.31.

51   *None of These Diseases: The Bible's Health Secrets for the 21ˢᵗ Century by S.S. McMillen, M.D. & David E. Stern, M.D. records a variety of practices taught in the Scripture that was contrary to the learning of the time but later discovered to be true.*

cloudy. Which one was correct? Both were. It all depended on which part of the sky I chose to focus on. When it is partly sunny it is at the same time partly cloudy. A glass half full is also a glass half empty. Most of what people call contradictions are nothing more than authors emphasizing different details. If all the Gospels used the same words and provided identical details, it would raise questions of collusion. Their accounts are strengthened by the fact that some of the details differ while not contradicting the accounts they report—as you would expect from eyewitness testimony.

You could dig into other points such as what some have deemed as counterproductive content, i.e., information you wouldn't include if you were making the account up. For instance, Peter's failures, the disciples' lack of faith, the first witnesses to the resurrection being women, whose testimonies were not legally valid at that time, all the failures of Israel, etc. The Bible records many unflattering details about "God's people" precisely because it is not fabricating a story but faithfully recounting one. Or, as some call it, His story.

MAN'S WORD OR GOD'S WORD?

Which gets to the heart of the matter. Our copies reflect the original documents, original documents that are proven trustworthy, but is it inspired by God? Paul professes, "[16] All Scripture is *breathed out by God* and profitable for teaching, for reproof, for correction, and for training in righteousness,".[52] Peter similarly stated,

> And we have the prophetic word more fully
> confirmed, to which you will do well to pay

---

52 2 Timothy 3:16.

attention as to a lamp shining in a dark place, until the day dawns and the morning star rises in your hearts, [20] knowing this first of all, that no prophecy of Scripture comes from someone's own interpretation. [21] For no prophecy was ever produced by the will of man, *but men spoke from God* as they were carried along by the Holy Spirit.[53]

Estimates vary, but the Bible directly or indirectly asserts its divine authorship over one thousand five hundred times. If the Bible lies about its authorship, it casts a shadow of doubt over its entire content. To assert to be God's word is an audacious claim unless it is true. We have already looked at the remarkable ways the Bible shows itself trustworthy as a historical record. What basis do we have for declaring it is more? Erwin Lutzer comments, "If the Bible is reliable in what we can observe, then it is reasonable to trust in matters that we can't."[54] I concur that this is a starting point, but it does take more to conclude this is God's word to us.

CONSISTENCY, FULFILLED PROPHECY, AND TRANSFORMATION

Consider that when Paul writes of the "holy Scriptures" he refers to not just one book, but a composite of books written over 1300-1500 years. And you thought those term papers took a long time to write. The Bible is composed of many books written by at least forty different authors from a great

---

53   2 Peter 1:19–21.
54   Erwin Lutzer, *Seven Reasons Why You Can Trust the Bible* (Moody Publishers, 2015). I used the quote in a past sermon and do not have a page number.

ethnic and geographical diversity and from various social and economic circumstances and walks of life. There are a variety of genres, as well as three different languages: Hebrew, Aramaic, and Greek. Yet, despite dealing with controversial issues, there is congruity, consistency, and coherence from Genesis to Revelation. "The fact that the Bible has unity despite obvious differences in content, style, and perspective is a powerful witness to the independence of each author... revealing no collusion."[55]

Several years ago, we had a major decision to make as a church. I took a few months to educate the congregation on all the facts before the big vote came. Our small congregation had a unanimous vote, which I have comically shared with others, "You know the definition of a miracle: a unanimous vote in a church." Even people from the same background and the same language struggle to all agree. Imagine added to the "miracle" of the consensus of diverse voices, over a couple thousand years, in three languages, the fulfillment of prophecy. The Bible is not only historically reliable, but it also reported history before it even happened. "Thirty percent of the Bible consists of prophecy, and not one of its prophecies has ever shown to be false... In the Old Testament alone, over two thousand prophecies have already come to pass."[56] Nevertheless, there is power not only in foretelling what will occur through prophecy but also in its message to transform individuals as well as entire cultures. *Unimaginable: What Our World Would Be Like Without Christianity* by Jeremiah Johnston underscores that you can't overstate the positive impact of Christianity on the world. While it is true that Christians have not always lived

---

55   Ibid.
56   Merritt, James. *God, I've Got a Question: Biblical Truth for Our Deepest Concerns*. Eugene, Oregon: Harvest House, 2011, p. 33.

up to their name, the world today owes a great deal of gratitude to the transforming power of the gospel message.

The Bible is remarkable in its preservation, historically accurate, scientifically insightful, astonishingly cohesive, and filled with fulfilled prophecies and life-transforming truth. Each of these would be deemed amazing in isolation from one another, but *cumulatively* they point to the Bible as God's word rather than simply a work of man. It is not merely man's words about God, but God's word revealed to and through man, so that you might come to know God and walk with Him.

However, God was not content with merely the written word. He chose to reveal Himself as the "Living Word" in the person of Jesus Christ. Before exploring what sets Him apart from every other religious figure in history, it is essential to first examine Him as a historical figure—a step that will deepen your understanding of His unparalleled significance and prepare you to answer: *why Jesus*?

Chapter 4

The Man Who Changed History

1 John 1:1-4

*To this day more than two billion people worldwide
claim to be followers [of Jesus], more than the number
of adherents to any other religion or worldview.
Christianity is responsible for a disproportionately
large number of the humanitarian advances in the
history of civilization—in education, medicine,
law, the fine arts, working for human rights, and
even the natural sciences (based on the belief that
God designed the universe in an orderly fashion
and left clues for people to learn about it.*[57]

No historical figure has had a greater impact than a carpenter
from Nazareth named Jesus. He did not enter history as a
mighty king or political figure; nonetheless, His life forever
changed the world. What can you know about Him?

---

57   Groothuis, Douglas. *Christian Apologetics: A Comprehensive Case for
Biblical Faith.* Downers Grove, IL: Intervarsity Press, 2011, chapter by Craig
Blomberg, p. 438.

THE HISTORICAL JESUS

Jesus stands not only at the center of Christianity but has such an impact on the world stage that every other major religion needs to recognize Him in some manner. J. Warner Wallace provides this summary of how some other religions handle the historical figure of Jesus. The Jews view Jesus as a teacher and miracle worker who claimed to be the Messiah and was crucified. Islam treats Jesus as a significant person, born of a virgin, revered as a prophet, wise teacher, miracle worker, and affirms His ascension to heaven, but denies Him as God or Son of God. Ahmadiyya teaches that Jesus was a prophet, wise teacher, and miracle worker, and as surviving the crucifixion. Bahai affirms that Jesus came from God, was born of a virgin, spoke for God, was a wise teacher and miracle worker with both a divine and human nature, who died and was spiritually, as opposed to bodily, resurrected. Hindus view Jesus as a holy man, a wise teacher, and a god, but not the one true God. Buddhism accepts Jesus as a holy man, a wise teacher, and as enlightened. New Age embraces Him as a wise moral teacher.[58]

Jesus' profound impact on the world is undeniable, compelling various religions to acknowledge Him in different ways. However, their claims about His identity often stand in direct contradiction to one another. Logically speaking, they could all be false, but they cannot all be true. Jesus can't be both the Son of God and not the Son of God; He can't have both physically risen from the grave and not physically risen from the grave after being crucified. From an apologetic standpoint, two key points must be verified (1) that Jesus of Nazareth physically existed in history—though some may

---

58 https://coldcasechristianity.com/writings/who-is-jesus-according-to-other-religions/, by J. Warner Wallace

deny His historicity, this view is largely dismissed considering overwhelming evidence—and (2) that the Bible, specifically the Gospels, is the most trustworthy source in revealing His identity. This is why the last chapter established the trustworthiness of the Bible.

Without a historical Jesus, Christianity would not exist, as it is a faith based in historical events—namely the life, death, and resurrection of Jesus. I realize I have not dealt with evidence for the resurrection yet. I will do that in chapter 5, but Paul would write, "And if Christ has not been raised, then our preaching is in vain and your faith is in vain."[59] Yet, before acknowledging the resurrection, you must first speak of the historical Jesus in general. John was one of the first followers of Jesus, and he wrote:

> That which was from the beginning, which we have heard, which we have seen with our eyes, which we looked upon and have touched with our hands, concerning the word of life— [2] the life was made manifest, and we have seen it, and testify to it and proclaim to you the eternal life, which was with the Father and was made manifest to us— [3] that which we have seen and heard we proclaim also to you, so that you too may have fellowship with us; and indeed our fellowship is with the Father and with his Son Jesus Christ. [4] And we are writing these things so that our joy may be complete.[60]

---

59 1 Corinthians 15:14.
60 1 John 1:1–4.

In the last chapter, we examined the accuracy of the written word with a nod to the "living word." John speaks of "the word of life," which was made manifest to us. He emphasizes how this "word of life" took on flesh with the language of "we have heard, which we have seen with our eyes, which we have looked upon and touched with our hands." He emphasizes how the Son of the Father took on flesh and dwelt among us.[61]

Unlike other religious leaders, Jesus did not simply teach a way of life—He claimed to be the way itself. Other religious leaders left behind teachings such as the Five Pillars, the Noble Eightfold Path, and the Four Noble Truths. But Jesus didn't merely provide a way to live—He claimed to be *the* way. Ravi Zacharias points out,

> It is not Zoroaster to whom you turn. It is Zoroaster to whom you listen. It is not Buddha who delivers you; it is his Noble Truths that instruct you. It is not Mohammad who transforms you; it is the beauty of the Koran that woos you. By contrast, Jesus did not only teach or expound His message. He was identical with His message. 'In Him,' say the Scriptures, 'dwelt the fullness of the Godhead bodily.' He did not just proclaim the truth. He said, 'I am the truth.' He did not just show a way. He said, 'I am the way.' He did not just open vistas. He said, 'I am the door." 'I am the Good Shepherd.' 'I am the resurrection and the life.' 'I am the I am.' [62]

---

61   See John 1:14

62   Zacharias, Ravi. *Jesus Among Other Gods: The Absolute Claims of the Christian Message*. Nashville, Tennessee: Word Publishing, 2000, p89. Zoroaster was an ancient Iranian prophet who founded. Zoroastrianism.

We will explore the claims that Jesus made regarding Himself in chapter 6, for now I will simply remind you that Christianity does not rise or fall with Christians but with Jesus, and that the Jesus of history cannot be divided from the Christ of faith for Christianity to stand.[63] This is vital as there are Gnostic materials that declare the descent of Christ was not *physical* but *spiritual*, that Jesus did not die in reality, but only in appearance. John emphasizes what they had heard, seen, and touched to contend with this false teaching of Gnosticism. This Jesus was not merely a spiritual being, but One Who had come in flesh and blood. None of the Jewish sources or rabbis of Jesus' time denied His physical existence. Rather, they used the events of Jesus' life against Him as "…his birth, ministry, and death occasioned claims that his birth was illegitimate and that he performed miracles by evil magic, encouraged apostasy and was justly executed for his own sins. But they do not deny his existence."[64]

GREATEST STORY EVER TOLD, OR GREATEST STORY EVER SOLD?

Jesus existed as a man in history. Some of you may be thinking, "duh." However, some allege that Christianity is either the greatest story ever told, or the greatest story ever sold. Some skeptics claim it is nothing more than a myth, an invention of the church. Never mind that there was nothing to be gained by inventing a story, which inevitably led to the persecution and martyrdom of many of the first followers. Part of the strength

---

63   Some have tried to separate the Christ of faith from the Jesus of history; however, Christianity is a faith based off the historical facts of Jesus.

64   https://www.biblicalarchaeology.org/daily/people-cultures-in-the-bible/jesus-historical-jesus/did-jesus-exist/, Lawrence Mykytiuk. If apostasy is a new term for you, it refers to renouncing one's previous faith.

of the New Testament, which is relayed to you in what was heard, seen, and touched, by John, is in that it was written by actual eyewitnesses and during a time when other eyewitnesses could either verify or challenge the details. In the last chapter, we established that the New Testament is a credible source of history. The New Testament authors needed to record an accurate history, or their opponents would have thrown it back in their faces. Written by eyewitnesses to eyewitnesses, details could easily be verified or contested.

It was not just the Christians who testified to the existence of Jesus, nor verified many of the details believed by Christians and reported in the New Testament. Josh McDowell offers an entire list of Roman historians, and a Jewish historian named Josephus, who provide evidence outside of the Bible for many details about the life, death, and believed resurrection of Jesus. From the writings of Josephus, we learn,

> Now there was about this time Jesus, a wise man, *if it be lawful to call him a man*, for he was a doer of wonderful works, a teacher of such men as receive the truth with pleasure. He drew over to him both many of the Jews, and many of the Gentiles. *He was the Christ*, and when Pilate, at the suggestion of the principal men among us, had condemned him to the cross, those that loved him at the first did not forsake him; *for he appeared to them alive again the third day; as the divine prophets had foretold these and ten thousand other wonderful things concerning him.* And the tribe of Christians so named from him are not

extinct at this day. (*Antiquities*, XVIII, 33, italics added).[65]

Craig Blomberg reports over a dozen or more references to Jesus in non-Christian, Jewish, Greek, and Roman sources that provide evidence for various historical facts about Jesus. He writes,

> It is, of course, historically prejudicial to exclude automatically all Christian evidence, as if no one who became a follower of Jesus could ever report accurately about his life and teachings, or to assume that all non-Christian evidence was necessarily more "objective." But even using only such non-Christian sources, there is ample evidence to confirm the main contours of the early Christian claims: Jesus was a Jew who lived in Israel during the first third of the first century, was born out of wedlock, intersected with the life and ministry of John the Baptist, attracted great crowds especially because of his wondrous deeds, had a group of particularly close followers called disciples (five of whom are named), ran afoul of the Jewish religious authorities because of his controversial teachings sometimes deemed heretical or blasphemous, was crucified during the time of Pontius Pilate's governorship in Judea (26–36 C.E.), and yet was believed by many of his followers to have been the Messiah, the anticipated liberator of Israel.

---

65   McDowell, J. (2006). *Evidence for Christianity* (pp. 177–178). Thomas Nelson Publishers.

This belief did not disappear despite Jesus' death because a number of his supporters claimed to have seen him resurrected from the dead. His followers, therefore, continued consistently to grow in numbers, gathering together regularly for worship and instruction and even singing hymns to him as if he were a god (or God).[66]

NOT A FISH STORY

With the abundance of references to Jesus from Roman, Jewish, pagan, and Christian sources, it is difficult, if not impossible, to deny His historical existence. But there is more. Jesus grew up in poverty, not a palace, in Nazareth, not a renowned city. He was a carpenter by trade and became rabbi, not a conquering political king. Why does Jesus show up in the writings of so many historians?

This raises an important question, not of His existence but Who He was. I don't know how many of you like fishing. Me, not so much; however, I have heard some fish stories. Why do fish stories seem to grow when they are told? How do you know that did not happen with Jesus? Jesus existed, but did Christians embellish His story? The answer to this question is why we started in the last chapter with the trustworthiness of Scripture and have highlighted the importance of understanding that the New Testament was entirely composed within the lifetime of eyewitnesses and far too early for legend and myth to develop.

---

66   Groothuis, Douglas. *Christian Apologetics: A Comprehensive Case for Biblical Faith.* Downers Grove, IL: Intervarsity Press, 2011, chapter by Craig Blomberg, p.439-440.

As I noted earlier in the chapter, it is not only Christianity but also world religions and history that must grapple with the identity of Jesus. If Jesus was Who He claimed to be, then eternity hangs in the balance. Logically, all the claims made of Jesus can be false, but contradicting one another they cannot all be true. This leaves you with, do you have reason to trust the account left to you in the Gospels?

Legends and myths take time to develop. However, the New Testament was written too soon after Jesus' life, death, and resurrection for embellishments to emerge. Even a liberal dating by liberal New Testament scholars placing the books of the New Testament at later dates still doesn't allow enough time for legend to develop. The Gospels are simply the oldest and best sources for knowing about the life of Jesus.

Concerning Luke's ability as a historian, Sir William Ramsay concluded after thirty years of study that "Luke is a historian of the first rank; not merely are his statements of fact trustworthy... this author should be placed along with the very greatest of historians" (Ramsay, BRDTNT, 222). Ramsay adds: "Luke's history is unsurpassed in respect of its trustworthiness" (Ramsay, SPTRC, 81). What Ramsay had done conclusively and finally was to exclude certain possibilities. As seen in the light of archaeological evidence, the New Testament reflects the conditions of the second half of the first century a.d. and does not reflect the conditions of any later date. Historically, it is of the greatest importance that this should have been so effectively established. In all matters of external fact, the author of Acts is seen to have been minutely careful and accurate as only a contemporary can be.[67]

WHAT MADE JESUS SUCH A DOMINANT FIGURE IN HISTORY?

What made Jesus not only a dominant figure in history but also One Whose influence endures two thousand years later? A man who hung on a cross would not have appealed to the Jew, nor the Gentile. Jews never would have made up an account of a crucified Messiah, and the Gentiles would have deemed it foolish to flock to someone who had hung on a Roman cross. Yet, historically, Jews and Gentiles not only began to follow Jesus but to worship Him immediately after His death. Why?

There was nothing to be gained by starting a new religion, while there was everything to lose. Christians were crucified, fed to wild animals, burned alive as torches for Nero's gardens, they suffered economic and physical persecution of all sorts. But even with everything to lose, their numbers rapidly grew. Why?

Jesus was not a politician. He was not a mighty general who won decisive military battles. It has been said that it is the victors that write history, but Jesus was crucified on the cross. Rejected by His people and crucified by Rome. Nonetheless, Jesus remains the most dominant figure in all history. What made this Jew from Nazareth have such power and influence over world history? Could the best answer be found in the doctrine of the resurrection, which heads the list of what sets Jesus apart from any other in answering, why Jesus?

---

67   McDowell, J. (2006). *Evidence for Christianity* (pp. 93–94). Thomas Nelson Publishers.

PART 2

WHY JESUS? BEYOND A REASONABLE DOUBT

Chapter 5

Alive Again

1 Corinthians 15

TRASH TALK

Before a big game, athletes and fans might engage in trash talk. They will talk big about the victory they will have over their opponent and how their opponent is sure to come up short. Of course, it is all talk until game time arrives. Game time will determine if they can back up their claims or find themselves "eating crow," humiliated in defeat despite previous boasting.

Before His ultimate test arrived, Jesus made some truly audacious predictions. Simply saying, "I'm going to die" is unremarkable. But declaring, "I will die and rise again"—now that is bold. "From that time Jesus began to show his disciples that he must go to Jerusalem and suffer many things from the elders and chief priests and scribes, and be killed, and on the third day be raised."[68] Jesus' prediction may not be the same as talking trash, but this outlandish prediction would either cause Him to "eat crow," or it would validate everything He said.

---

68 Matthew 16:21.

There are a variety of passages where Jesus foretold that He would die and rise again. On this occasion, in the next verse, Peter began to rebuke Jesus regarding the necessity of His suffering and death. Scholars note that skeptics struggle to dispute the authenticity of such a text because highlighting the failures of Jesus' disciples, the church's first leaders, enhances Scripture's credibility. If I were to make up a story, I wanted you to believe, I wouldn't start by exposing all my faults and failures. Making the initial leaders look bad is no way to amass a great following.

Jesus did not cop out by predicting a spiritual resurrection, which nobody can prove or disprove. However, a physical resurrection is a game-changer, as it can be easily disproven. All that is necessary is to produce the body. When game time comes, and the buzzer sounds, there either is or isn't a body to determine the victor. Enemies zero, Jesus won!

THE EMERGENCE OF THE CHURCH

Part 1 established some foundations for the reasonableness of faith in God, the trustworthiness of the Bible, and the historic person of Jesus. Yet, Christianity rises or falls on the resurrection of Jesus. In a world with so many different teachers, a plethora of diverse religions, and the mindset of many that what you believe doesn't matter if you believe in something, you are confronted with the question, why Jesus? The resurrection is the first and final answer to why Jesus, if it is true.

Scholars have posited that the resurrection of Jesus is a major historical problem. On the one hand, modern people want to deny miracles; on the other hand, if you disbelieve the resurrection of Jesus, you have difficulty explaining the emergence of the church and its rapid growth despite all that stood against it. "The institution of the church, ... is a historical phenomenon explained only by Jesus' resurrection."[69] Any attempt to explain away the resurrection must provide an alternative explanation for the origin of the church and those who gave their lives to proclaim that Jesus rose.

The first believers to follow Jesus were religious Jews. What occurred that would cause faithful Jews to change Sabbath worship to Sunday worship?[70] I jokingly say at church that I can take attendance with my eyes closed. Just tell me which seats are occupied. People are opposed to change, and if you think that changing where you sit in church is hard, keep in mind what a *big* deal Sabbath observance was to the Jews. Yet, Jewish believers in Jesus not only began to worship on Sunday but likewise proclaimed a crucified Messiah, contrary to all expectations of the time. They directed their worship to Jesus and were willing to die defending Jesus' resurrection.

A willingness to die for the message does not prove the resurrection but confirms their conviction that it was true. People will die for a lie, but not for what they know to be a lie. This is why it is critical to remember the shortness of time between Jesus' death and the emergence of those proclaiming His resurrection and giving Him worship.

It was absolute blasphemy to propose that any human being should be worshipped. Yet hundreds of Jews began worshipping Jesus overnight. The hymn to Christ as God that Paul

---

69   McDowell, J. (2006). *Evidence for Christianity* (p. 315). Thomas Nelson Publishers.
70   Sabbath ran from Friday evening to Saturday evening and was strictly observed by faithful Jews. Yet, followers of Christ began worshipping on Sunday, the day the empty tomb was discovered.

quotes in Philippians 2 is generally recognized to have been written just a few years after the crucifixion. What enormous event broke through all of that Jewish resistance?[71]

Of course, the emergence of the church is not the only reason to believe in the resurrection of Jesus, however, the emergence and the rapid growth of the church is best explained by the resurrection of Jesus.

AN EARLY CHRISTIAN CREED

Both Christian and non-Christian historians recognize 1 Corinthians 15 as an early and authentic historical document, with its writing typically dated between AD 53 and 56. However, in 1 Corinthians 15 Paul quotes from what is believed to be the earliest Christian creed:

> For I delivered to you as of first importance what I also received: that Christ died for our sins in accordance with the Scriptures, [4] that he was buried, that he was raised on the third day in accordance with the Scriptures, [5] and that he appeared to Cephas, then to the twelve.[72]

This creed is dated from just a few months to within a couple of years after the resurrection and reflects early Christian teaching, that Jesus died for your sins, was buried, and raised.

Some have suggested that Jesus never truly died on the cross. One of the oldest theories is that Jesus only appeared

---

71   Keller, Timothy. *The Reason for God: Belief in an Age of Skepticism.* New York, New York: Penguin Group, 2009), p218.
72   1 Corinthians 15:3–5.

to die and then be resuscitated in the tomb. Really? Have you ever undergone major surgery? Would you have been strong enough to turn around and push a huge boulder out of the way just days afterward? What Jesus endured went far beyond any major surgery and any theories that He only appeared to die, denies historical evidence and refuses to acknowledge the proficiency of the Romans in killing people.[73] Christians, skeptics, and atheists alike, who take history seriously, accept the preponderance of evidence pointing to Jesus being crucified and dying on the cross.

In addition, crucifixion was not only an excruciating way to die but carried with it a considerable stigma that would have appalled both Jews and Gentiles. In the movie *Meet the Robinsons*, there's a humorous scene where a dinosaur struggles—and hilariously fails—to capture Lewis. In response, the T-Rex quips something to the effect of, "I have a big head and little arms. I am just not sure how well this plan was thought through." If you were to invent a new religion, it would not start with a crucified leader. That plan would not be well thought through unless there was more to the story.

WHAT HAPPENED NEXT?

Undisputed historical facts point to Jesus' death. The difficulty for skeptics is that there is also strong evidence for the empty tomb, along with the myriad eyewitness accounts testifying to having seen the risen Jesus. The key historical question isn't whether Jesus died, but how to explain what happened next. What caused a movement that forever changed history?

---

73   *The Case of Christ* by Lee Strobel is an excellent work walking you through a journalist's investigation of the evidence for Jesus. If you would like to dig deeper, this would be a good read in examining the evidence.

As the early creed attests, "He was buried." Matthew records,

> When it was evening, there came a rich man from Arimathea, named Joseph, who also was a disciple of Jesus. [58] He went to Pilate and asked for the body of Jesus. Then Pilate ordered it to be given to him. [59] And Joseph took the body and wrapped it in a clean linen shroud [60] and laid it in his own new tomb, which he had cut in the rock. And he rolled a great stone to the entrance of the tomb and went away. [61] Mary Magdalene and the other Mary were there, sitting opposite the tomb. [74]

From Mark, you also learn that Joseph was a member of the council that condemned Jesus. Luke adds that he was a good and upright man who had not consented to their decision. John also speaks of Joseph, remarking that he came secretly to Pilate because he feared the Jews, and that the tomb in which they laid Jesus was close at hand.

All four Gospels refer to Joseph of Arimathea coming to ask for and burying the body of Jesus. You are also told that Pilate only released the body after verifying that Jesus was dead. Keep in mind that Jesus did not predict a spiritual but physical resurrection. In other words, all his enemies had to do was produce His body. Apart from an empty tomb, Jesus would have been "eating crow"; humiliated that His prediction had not come true. Matthew records that the religious leaders bribed the guards to say that the disciples stole the body; however, that would mean that the disciples were willing to

---

74   Matthew 27:57–61.

suffer greatly and die for something they knew to be a lie and without anything to gain. The idea that the disciples stole the body and then knowingly and willingly suffered and died for a lie doesn't hold up to any honest examination and is disproven by the sincerity of their conviction. Likewise, Jesus' enemies never denied the tomb was empty, rather they tried to concoct a story to create a false narrative.

Some have suggested that the body was thrown into a mass grave, or that burial was not allowed, but once again, if that were true then it could have been used by Jesus' enemies. It wasn't.

It is clear from the early laws and opinions cited in the *Digesta* that in most cases the bodies of the executed, including those crucified, were permitted burial, if requests were made. We see this in the case of Jesus, whose body for burial was requested by Joseph of Arimathea, a member of the Jewish council (Mark 15:42–47 parr.). This is completely consistent with Jewish law and custom, which placed the burden of burial on the Jewish council (or Sanhedrin) when it condemned and executed someone.[75]

Similarly, Christians would not have made a hero of a member of the Sanhedrin that condemned Jesus, unless they were reporting historical details.

What if the women went to the wrong tomb? While it is true that they did not have GPS and Google Maps in those days, this, like many alternative theories, is grasping for straws

75   https://hc.edu/news-and-events/2016/05/04/craig-evans-resurrection-je-sus-light-jewish-burial-p-ractices/

and fails to stand up under investigation. The tomb was nearby, and even if the women went to the wrong tomb, all Jesus' enemies had to do was go to the right one to disprove the resurrection. Its whereabouts were well known, and the religious leaders even posted a guard to keep it secure.[76] An empty tomb with no witnesses would not have led people to faith; likewise, witnesses without an empty tomb would quickly have been proven false.

EMPTY HOW?

The Christian creed then professes, "He was raised on the third day." A physically raised Jesus is dependent on a tomb without a body. Gary Habermas, who is viewed as an expert regarding the resurrection, lists just a few of the more than twenty arguments cited in favor of the empty tomb. The location near Jerusalem, women being the first witnesses, multiple independent sources attesting to the empty tomb, early preaching focused on the empty tomb, the lack of reverence or veneration for Jesus' tomb, common knowledge of the empty tomb, the Jewish response to the empty tomb, and the tradition of the empty tomb being very early.[77] Similarly, the simplicity with which the resurrection is recorded contrasts with the development of myths and legends. Myths and legends take time to evolve, over which details expand, get exaggerated, and become farther removed from actual history. The resurrection of Jesus, however, is recorded by eyewitnesses, far too early for myth and legend to grow, and unlike myths and legends, remarkable with its simplicity in

---

76   Matthew 27:62-66
77   Habermas, Gary. *Evidence for God: 50 Arguments for Faith from the Bible, History, Philosophy, and Science.* Ed by William A. Dembski and Michael R. Licona. Grand Rapids, Michigan: Baker Books, 2010, p169-171.

detail. All indicators accord with a credible account of history. Those who deny the resurrection do so based on theological or philosophical assumptions rather than an evaluation and best explanation for the evidence.

To recap, Jesus was crucified, which made for a very dead Jesus. He was buried in a known tomb, which then became empty. How? Explanations such as He only appeared to die, then revived, women going to the wrong tomb, or the disciples stealing the body are easily overturned as unsatisfactory theories to account for what is historically known. Another theory suggests that grave robbers were responsible, but upon closer examination, this idea is stripped of any merit. Not only does it fail to account for the posted guards, but it also overlooks a crucial detail—the tomb wasn't completely empty. The linens and face cloth, which would have contained the valuable burial spices, remained untouched inside.[78] That would mean grave robbers would have somehow circumvented the guards, taken time to strip the body, carried out a naked body, and left the only thing of monetary value in the tomb, robbing that theory of any merit.

Many propose alternative explanations for the empty tomb. Yet, like trash talk before a game, they collapse under investigation.

Winfried Corduan comments on the alternative theories to the Resurrection en masse: 'Non-miraculous explanations of what happened at the empty tomb have to face a cruel choice: either they have to rewrite the evidence in order to suit themselves or they have to accept the fact that they are not consistent with present evidence.

---

78   See John 20:1-10.

The only hypothesis that fits the evidence is that Jesus was really resurrected. Could the Man who predicted His death and resurrection, only to have it come to pass exactly as He had said, be anything but God?' (Corduan, NDA, 227).[79]

BEYOND THE EMPTY TOMB

The events of history, the witness of the disciples, and the silence of alternate answers add up to a solid case for the resurrection as the best explanation for the empty tomb. However, it was not an empty tomb alone that convinced the disciples of the resurrection. Following the recital of the creed, Paul wrote,

> and that [Jesus] appeared to Cephas, then to the twelve. [6] Then he appeared to more than five hundred brothers at one time, most of whom are still alive, though some have fallen asleep. [7] Then he appeared to James, then to all the apostles. [8] Last of all, as to one untimely born, he appeared also to me.[80]

Paul's list is not exhaustive as he leaves out the first witnesses, the women. If you were to examine all the resurrection narratives, you would discern that they highlight differences in secondary details but agree on the primary details. Many scholars emphasize how this is a strong case for credibility as it is what you would expect from authentic eyewitness accounts. If the story were told precisely in the

---

79 McDowell, J. (2006). *Evidence for Christianity* (pp. 315–316). Thomas Nelson Publishers.

80 1 Corinthians 15:5–8.

same way with the same words, it would show collusion rather than a credible witness.

Scholars point out that the resurrection narratives are trustworthy when judged by the critical methods of historical study applied to all ancient writings. Because they contain unflattering content portraying the disciples as scared and slow to believe, even exposing Thomas as a doubter, this suggests that they are not fabrications. There was no precedent for this in the ancient world.[81]

The undisputed historical facts are difficult to explain apart from Jesus' bodily resurrection:

- Defeated followers transformed overnight into bold witnesses.
- Worship shifted from Sabbath (Friday evening to Saturday evening) to Sunday.
- Women—who lacked legal standing as witnesses— were listed as the first witnesses.
- Despite being crucified, Jesus was declared Lord, by Jews and Gentiles alike.
- Monotheistic Jews who believed in one God began to worship Jesus.
- The rapid spread of the gospel and growth of the church despite heavy persecution.

---

81   Clark, Mark. *The Problem of God: Answering a Skeptic's Challenges to Christianity.* Grand Rapids, Michigan: Zondervan, 2017, p240.

The empty tomb did not stand alone. Coupled with appearances of Jesus, it was not merely those who previously followed Him that proclaimed the resurrection. Skeptics, like Jesus' brother James, converted. Antagonists such as Saul, who became known as the apostle Paul, converted. The conversion of former antagonists and skeptics eliminates the notion that the disciples merely experienced wishful-thinking hallucinations. Furthermore, multiple appearances—including one witnessed by over five hundred people at once—reinforce the credibility of these events.

THE IMPROBABLE TRUTH

But the resurrection defies science! So does the origin of the universe, somehow something came out of nothing. Once you accept the reality of God (chapter 1), is it so hard to accept the possibility of miracles? Jesus died, was buried, was raised, and then appeared to His followers and others. When you eliminate all other possibilities, whatever remains, however improbable, must be the truth. Oxford University professor, Richard Swinburne, is noted for his aptitude in evaluating evidence.

> In *The Resurrection of God Incarnate* Swinburne argues that the available evidence makes it overwhelmingly likely that Jesus was God incarnate who rose from the dead. More specifically, he argues that given our evidence, the probability that Jesus was God incarnate who rose from the dead is very high, somewhere around .97. Swinburne's argument is based on an application of Bayes' theorem, and most of the

book is support for the probability values he uses in that theorem.[82]

Someone may look at the evidence and concede the case can be made for the resurrection, 97% probability is highly probable, but then ask, why is that relevant to me? How does a Middle Eastern man rising from the dead two thousand years ago impact my life today? Fair question. First, Paul writes that "Christ died for our sins" (1 Corinthians 15:3). His death secures your forgiveness so that you might have fellowship with God. Similarly, His resurrection is the foundation for faith (1 Corinthians 15:12ff), it is described as the "firstfruits of those who have fallen asleep" (15:20), how you also can share in the resurrection of the dead (15:21-22) receive a resurrection body, and share in the kingdom of God, as death is swallowed up in victory (15:35ff). If that isn't enough, there is more. I am limiting myself to 1 Corinthians 15. Jesus' resurrection means your life can have meaning that death does not destroy.

WHY JESUS?

You may or may not agree with the Bible on many points; start with examining the evidence for the resurrection.[83] If it is false, then nothing else matters. Death awaits you and life is ultimately meaningless. However, if the resurrection of Jesus is true, then nothing matters more than what you believe about Jesus. Life has meaning that extends beyond the grave. All it costs you is a little time to investigate the greatest truth of all time.

---

82   https://ndpr.nd.edu/reviews/the-resurrection-of-god-incarnate/
83   I have only presented you with the tip of the iceberg. If you want more evidence for the resurrection, I recommend *The Case of Christ* by Lee Strobel or *Evidence that Demands a Verdict* by Josh McDowell.

Why Jesus? The resurrection seems to be a good starting point. It is the first and final answer to why you should place your faith in Jesus and follow Him.

Thomas Arnold was for fourteen years the famous headmaster of Rugby, author of the famous three-volume *History of Rome*, appointed to the chair of modern history at Oxford, and certainly a man well acquainted with the value of evidence in determining historical facts. Speaking of the evidence for Christ's resurrection, this great scholar remarked:

"Thousands and tens of thousands of persons have gone through it piece by piece, as carefully as every judge summing up on a most important case. I have myself done it many times over, not to persuade others but to satisfy myself. I have been used for many years to study the histories of other times, and to examine and weigh the evidence of those who have written about them, and I know of no one fact in the history of mankind which is proved by better and fuller evidence of every sort, to the understanding of a fair inquirer, than the great sign which God hath given us that Christ died and rose again from the dead." (Arnold, as cited in Smith, TS, 425–26).[84]

You may talk trash and razz one another regarding your sports, but the resurrection is not about winning or losing a game and moving on. It is about life, death, and eternity. Once

---

84 McDowell, J. (2006). *Evidence for Christianity* (pp. 262–263). Thomas Nelson Publishers.

the buzzer sounds it is too late. Why Jesus? The resurrection is
the exclamation point for why, but let's investigate the build-up
to His death and resurrection as we build our case.

Chapter 6

His Claims

Mark 14:53-65

TABOO TOPICS

When I was in high school, a group of friends and I played a game of Taboo. If you are unfamiliar with Taboo, you break up into teams, and you have one person on your team trying to get his or her teammates to guess a particular word before time runs out. However, certain words are off-limits as hints. One player struggled to get their teammates to guess the word and in desperation his final hint was, "I am …". Talk about opening a dangerous door.

The guesses began to fly—arrogant, egotistical, conceited, nerd, geek…. I don't remember what else. As time expired, he commented: "Now I know what you think of me. The word was 'hunk!'" Obviously how he viewed himself differed a bit from how others saw him. While I can appreciate his strong self-confidence, "hunk" might have been stretching it, in my humble opinion.

I wonder what hints people might give if they were trying to get people to guess the name Jesus.

THE CENTRAL QUESTION: WHO IS JESUS?

What turned out to be a fun moment of my past illustrates three things you must consider about identity. The first is how a person views themself. The second is how others perceive you, and the third is whether those views reflect reality. This chapter and the next chapter must be held together, as it is one thing to allege something of myself and another for my life to back up that claim.

In high school, I used to go out into the driveway to shoot baskets, pretending to be Michael Jordan. It just happened that I was always making the game-winning shot. Of course, if I missed that meant I was fouled and I went to the free throw line to win the game. It was fun to pretend I was the greatest player of all time, so long as I didn't believe it—because the facts wouldn't support that belief. Many people might suffer from a "messiah complex;" yet that can only be true of those who are not the Messiah.[85]

The Scriptures instruct you to view yourself rightly, not too highly nor too lowly, but honestly.[86] As you investigate Who Jesus is, you must address what Jesus said of Himself. It may feel as though you are moving backward considering that you explored reasons to believe in the resurrection of Jesus in the last chapter; however, this and the next chapter will help you see what precipitated Jesus' crucifixion. Think of it like a TV show that begins with a scene and then takes you back to see how the characters got there. The challenge posed by the New Testament witness is not so much what Jesus taught, nor what Jesus did, but Who is Jesus, and what is His relevance to you.

---

85   Messiah is the Hebrew for "anointed one." The Greek equivalent is "Christ."
86   See Romans 12:3

JESUS ON TRIAL

Mark 14:53-65 takes you to Jesus' trial before the Sanhedrin, the Jewish ruling council. However, this was a unique trial.

> Irwin Linton, a lawyer, brings this out when he states, 'Unique among criminal trials is this one in which not the actions but the identity of the accused is the issue. The criminal charge laid against Christ, the confession or testimony or, rather, act in presence of the court, on which He was convicted, the interrogation by the Roman governor and the inscription and proclamation on His cross at the time of execution all are concerned with the one question of Christ's real identity and dignity. 'What think ye of Christ? Whose son is he?' (Linton, SV, 7).[87]

The world does not debate Jesus' historical existence, His teachings, or His impact on history. What has always divided people is His identity. Who was this man, whose influence endures to this day? Was He merely a good man, a wise teacher, a moral example, a prophet, or was He more? To answer these questions, you must start by examining how Jesus saw Himself and how others perceived Him. As you read through the gospels you will encounter various viewpoints including that Jesus was crazy, demonized, a blasphemer, as well as the Son of God Who is to be worshipped. Part of the authenticity and credibility of Scripture is that it includes all these diverse

---

87   McDowell, J. (2006). *Evidence for Christianity* (p. 354). Thomas Nelson Publishers.

viewpoints of what people thought, but what people thought doesn't change what is true.

I happen to be an identical twin. I cannot tell you how often people have mistaken me for my brother Dave. There have been times when people thought I was rude when I failed to recognize someone I never met, or even thought I was committing adultery when they saw who they thought was me with the wrong lady. I received a hug and a squeeze of the cheeks once for him with, "I can't thank you enough for all you have done for me," from a young lady I had never met before.

All sorts of people have opinions regarding who they think Jesus may or may not be, opinions all of which cannot be correct. Secular history agrees with the New Testament, in that Jesus lived and was worshipped as God very early. The question is not was He worshipped as God, but instead, is He *deserving* of worship as God. Was Jesus "guilty" of being Who He claimed to be? Who did He claim to be?

JESUS' CLAIMS

Thomas Schultz pointed out that

> Not one religious leader, not Moses, Paul, Buddha, Mohammed, Confucious, etc., has ever claimed to be God; that is, with the exception of Jesus Christ. Christ is the only religious leader who has ever claimed to be deity and the only individual ever who has convinced a great portion of the world that He is God.[88]

---

88   I could not find the source from when I included this quote in a sermon as I worked through many books at the time. In searching online, I discovered that Schultz is often quoted in various works.

The world is not divided over the existence of Jesus, but His identity. Josh McDowell includes this chart in his book, *Evidence that Demands a Verdict*, that helps explore the options available to us based on the claims Jesus made.

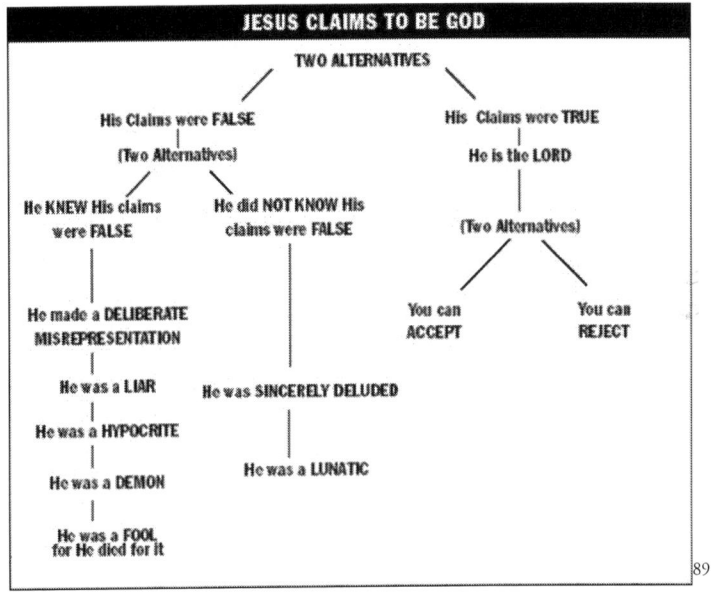

This chart presupposes that Jesus claimed to be God. If He did, then He was either a liar—deliberately deceiving people—a lunatic, mistakenly believing He was God, or He was telling the truth and really was, and still is, the Son of God. Some have critiqued the trilemma argument for not exploring all possible scenarios. They might allege that Jesus never made such claims, and that these claims grew out of legend or stemmed from misinterpretations of what He said. However, we have already established the historical reliability of the New Testament, as well as the fact that it was written

89   McDowell, J. (2017). *Evidence that Demands a Verdict* (p. 197). Thomas Nelson Publishers.

too soon for legends to develop (see chapter 2). Additionally, there is historical evidence for early Christian martyrdom and the rapid spread of Christianity, which makes the "legend" hypothesis less plausible. Similarly, it was not only what Jesus asserted, but also the actions He took—such as forgiving sins—that reinforced His claims. These claims were not only promoted by His disciples but also verified by the charges leveled against Him by His enemies.

We will explore what Jesus claimed here and then ask the related question in the next chapter. Did He back up His claims?

WHAT WAS JESUS' CRIME?

Why was Jesus on trial and what was He condemned for? "Now the chief priests and the whole council were seeking testimony against Jesus to put him to death, but they found none. [56] For many bore false witness against him, but their testimony did not agree."[90] Jesus lived in such a way that even false testimony could not condemn Him. Turns out when there are those giving false testimonies, it was harder for them to line up with all their witnesses. However, there was some consistent testimony regarding Jesus:

- Judas saying, "I have sinned by betraying innocent blood."[91]
- Pilate saying to the chief priests and the crowds, "I find no guilt in this man."[92]
- Pilate then called together the chief priests and the rulers and the people, [14] and said to them, "You

---

90   Mark 14:55–56.
91   Matthew 27:4.
92   Luke 23:4.

brought me this man as one who was misleading the people. And after examining him before you, behold, I did not find this man guilty of any of your charges against him. **¹⁵** Neither did Herod, for he sent him back to us. Look, nothing deserving death has been done by him.⁹³

- "One of the thieves crucified next to Jesus, saying,] And we indeed justly [are being punished], for we are receiving the due reward of our deeds; but this man has done nothing wrong."⁹⁴

- Now when the centurion saw what had taken place, he praised God, saying, "Certainly this man was innocent!"⁹⁵

Jesus was on trial and would be convicted not for a crime committed but a claim made. The turning point of His trial was not with irrefutable evidence from one of the "witnesses," but with Jesus' response to the high priest.

> **⁶¹** But he remained silent and made no answer. Again the high priest asked him, "Are you the Christ, the Son of the Blessed?" **⁶²** And Jesus said, "I am, and you will see the Son of Man seated at the right hand of Power, and coming with the clouds of heaven." **⁶³** And the high priest tore his garments and said, "What further witnesses do we need? **⁶⁴** You have heard his blasphemy. What

---

93   Luke 23:13–15.
94   Luke 23:41.
95   Luke 23:47.

is your decision?" And they all condemned him as deserving death.[96]

Jesus was charged with blasphemy for Whom He claimed to be.

Understanding how Jesus' statements were interpreted in His time is crucial, especially since some today argue that He never claimed to be God. They insist, "Jesus never claimed to be God—that was a later invention of the church." However, the charges made against Jesus overrule that assumption, "You have heard his blasphemy". Jesus' response affirmed that He was claiming to be the Christ. Contrary to how you may hear Jesus' name used on the streets, Christ is not His last name but a title which means "anointed one." "The Son of the Blessed" was a way of speaking of the Son of God without using the name of God. Jesus affirmed these titles from the high priest's question and added to them.

He not only claimed to be the Christ and the Son of the Blessed, but also the "Son of Man." Big deal you might think. Until you realize that "Son of Man" was a loaded title taken from the Old Testament book of Daniel.[97] "You will see the Son of Man seated at the right hand of Power, and coming with the clouds of heaven," sounds like pretty big talk. In the Old Testament, God appeared in the clouds, and Jesus' claim to divinity was unmistakable. Through their charge of blasphemy, they confirmed the claims Jesus was making of Himself to be God, which you will explore more in later chapters, especially chapter 10.

---

96   Mark 14:61–64.
97   See Daniel 9:7-14.

IT'S ONLY BLASPHEMY IF UNTRUE

If Jesus' enemies understood what Jesus was saying about Himself, why do people today say that Jesus never claimed to be God? If they acknowledge that He did, then Jesus—and Christianity—stand uniquely apart from all other religions. They would prefer Jesus had never made this claim, as it challenges the notion that all religions are equal. It would challenge the assumption that it doesn't matter what you believe, only that you believe something. Truth has become a casualty in the pursuit of consensus. Keep in mind that what Jesus said was blasphemy, only if untrue. You must weigh what Jesus claimed in conjunction with what Jesus did (next chapter), if you want to come to terms with Who Jesus is.

Time for another flashback as the road to Jesus' trial was paved with many such claims as Jesus both directly and indirectly made statements that you must come to terms with.

DIRECT CLAIMS

Jesus was understood to be making Himself equal with God in the work that He was doing[98] as well as boldly stating that "before Abraham was born, I am!" [99] Incidentally, this statement led them to pick up stones to throw at Him per the Old Testament way of handling a blasphemer. The phrase "I am" directly links to God's self-identification to Moses at the burning bush.[100] As for Abraham—he lived long before Moses. I understand that for those of you who have crossed fifty years old, you may begin to feel that you are "older than dirt", but Jesus literally professes to be older than dirt. He asserts that

---

98   See John 5:17-18
99   John 8:58.
100   Exodus 3:14.

before He existed as a son of man He existed as the Son of God. Jesus likewise alleged to be one with the Father and that anyone who had seen Him had seen the Father,[101] and that is just the tip of the iceberg.

So far, I have limited myself to the Gospel of John and only given you a small sampling of statements by Jesus regarding how He viewed Himself. I began with John because some argue that he was the last Gospel writer and that his account portrays the highest view of Jesus. However, Matthew and Luke both record a virgin conceiving by the Holy Spirit. That doesn't sound normal to me but rather prepares you for One unlike any other, which is affirmed as you read through the Gospels and discover in Jesus' statements that He uniquely knows and reveals the Father, inviting you to believe in and come to Him.[102]

INDIRECT CLAIMS

What John states explicitly, the Gospels—Matthew, Mark, and Luke—convey just as powerfully, though more indirectly. Jesus didn't claim to abolish the Law but to fulfill it, repeatedly declaring, "It is written, but I say to you." Unlike the rabbis of His day, who grounded their authority in tradition and traced it back to the Torah, Jesus spoke with an authority all His own. His words—"It is written, but I say to you"—implied nothing less than authority over the Torah itself.

Depending on your translation, Jesus prefaced statements with "Amen, Amen...I tell you the truth...Most Assuredly... Verily, verily." "Jesus' sense of authority, sincerity, and certainty

---

101   See John 10:30, 14:9.
102   See Matthew 11:25-30. It is significant that Jesus invites people to come to Him rather than to the Father, for it is in coming to Jesus that you come to the Father.

are demonstrated in his frequent use of *amen* before making a statement. This form of address is found in all the Gospels but was never used by anyone but Jesus."[103] Jesus did not wait for others to confirm the truthfulness of what He said but expected others to receive what He said as truth.

Jesus claimed authority to forgive sins, authority that belonged to God alone,[104] included Himself in some of the parables that He taught, and repeatedly referred to Himself as having come or been sent from heaven,[105] as well as referred to Himself as not only the Lord of the Sabbath,[106] but as the One to Whom judgment belonged.[107] By claiming authority over the law, given by God, calling Himself the Lord of the Sabbath, instituted by God, and possessing the power to forgive sins, the prerogative of God; Jesus claimed, "I am God" in a myriad of ways.

These indirect and direct claims equated to blasphemy if they were not true. What may escape your notice at Jesus' trial certainly did not escape theirs. Jesus affirms He is the Christ, the Son of the Blessed One, the Son of Man from Daniel's vision. He also alludes to the Messianic prophecy from Psalm 110:1, through the language of being seated by the right hand of Power. "Coming with the clouds" was Old Testament language attributed to God, all culminating in the charge of blasphemy. There is a saying, if it looks like a duck, quacks like a duck, and swims like a duck, it is a duck. Jesus'

---

103   Groothuis, Douglas. *Christian Apologetics: A Comprehensive Case for Biblical Faith.* Downers Grove, IL: Intervarsity Press, 2011, p. 490.
104   See Mark 2:1-12.
105   See for example Matt. 10:40, 15:24, 23:27; Mark 9:37; Luke 9:48, 10:16, 13:34; John 5, 6, 8, 10, 12, 17, and 20. This is not exhaustive but enough to illustrate the point.
106   Mark 12:8, Luke 6:5.
107   Matthew 16:24-27, 25:31-46. Not exhaustive just illustrative.

assertions could not have been clearer, confronting you not so much with what He said, but whether what He said was true.

MINIMAL FACTS, MAXIMUM RESULT

Gary Habermas and Royce Gruenler took a 'minimal facts' subset of the claims of the New Testament.

> 'Minimal facts' are a subset of the factual claims of the New Testament, consisting of the texts that even the most radical New Testament critics believe to be authentic These texts alone attest that Jesus made extraordinary claims about himself…but even given this overly stringent filter, these sayings show that Jesus deemed himself greater than any previous or future religious figure and that he believed he possessed the very authority of God to declare forgiveness of sins, to judge the world at the end of history and even to receive worship.[108]

Incidentally, this same approach likewise establishes the core of the gospel as expressed in the early Christian creed we looked at in the last chapter: that Jesus died by crucifixion, was buried in a known tomb, the tomb was found empty, and there were postmortem appearances of Jesus.[109]

You have examined Jesus' claims about Himself—claims His enemies confirmed through their accusations and His disciples professed as true.

---

108   Groothuis, Douglas. *Christian Apologetics: A Comprehensive Case for Biblical Faith*. Downers Grove, IL: Intervarsity Press, 2011, p.476.
109   Ibid, p.539-550.

William Biederwolf draws from the evidence a very apt comparison: "A man who can read the New Testament and not see that Christ claims to be more than a man, can look all over the sky at high noon on a cloudless day and not see the sun" (Mead, ERQ, 50).[110]

The first Christians were Jews who began referring to Jesus as Lord and worshipping Him, practically overnight. The resurrection is the most compelling explanation for this transformation powerfully validating the claims examined in this chapter.

OPINIONS ARE A DIME A DOZEN

Opinions are a dime a dozen; everyone has one but that doesn't make it right. You can find all sorts of ideas on the internet, but being on the internet doesn't make it true. As my friend discovered in Taboo, people have opinions about who they think you are (or in this case, who they think Jesus is). Some of those opinions may be true, others not so much; the question is which opinions are confirmed with evidence to support them?

Jesus' enemies and His disciples both heard His claims; however, they came to different interpretations. His enemies charged Him with blasphemy while others called Him Lord. As the earlier chart illustrated, the claims that Jesus made of Himself do not leave us with the option of merely a great moral teacher. Based on His own claims, Jesus was either a liar, a lunatic, or He is Lord. When you weigh the evidence, liar and lunatic do not fit with what we otherwise know of Jesus' life

---

110   McDowell, J. (2006). *Evidence for Christianity* (p. 374). Thomas Nelson Publishers.

and teachings which led His disciples to the conclusion that He was and is Lord.

None of you are exempt from asking, "Who is Jesus?" It is the most important question you can answer. His claims of divinity were confirmed through His resurrection, but even before that they were reinforced by a man who lived like no other. Jesus' big talk was reinforced with a big walk as we turn next to the life He lived.

Chapter 7

His Life

John 10:22-39

DID HIS WALK MATCH HIS TALK?

I became a grandfather on June 3, 2021. Before that, I became a father on April 2, 2001. Before that, I became a husband on August 12, 1995, when I said, "I do." Even before that, I became a son and a brother, on January 31, 1974. Before that, I was being uniquely fashioned and knit together in my mother's womb.[111] Before that, well, I was nothing, and that is enough of that.

In the previous chapter, we explored the identity of Jesus—examining how it encompasses self-perception, others' perceptions, and the reality of who He truly is. Unfortunately, self-perception is subject to self-deception. We all know someone who talks bigger than they deliver. Likewise, you have likely experienced the rigorous exercise of jumping to conclusions and perhaps backpedaling after realizing you were wrong about someone or something. Over time, truth emerges as new observations continually shape and refine perceptions.

---

111   Psalm 139:13-16.

Anyone can talk big. The question is not whether you can talk big but if you can deliver. In the last chapter, we explored Jesus' claims. Now we must ask, "Did His walk match His talk?" Did He deliver?

WHAT WE DO SPEAKS TO WHO WE ARE

Part of your identity, like it or not, is defined by your relationships with others, such as my being a grandfather, a father, a husband, a son, and a brother. Some of you either benefited or suffered from having an older sibling in school. You lived in their shadow and were prejudged based on who you were related to. Jesus' claims often included how He identified Himself relationally to the Father, in ways uncommon among Jews at the time:

- The works that I do in my Father's name…
- No one will snatch them out of My hand. My Father, who has given them to Me is greater than all, and no one is able to snatch them out of the Father's hand.
- I and the Father are one.
- Shown you good works from the Father…
- Of Him Whom the Father consecrated and sent into the world…
- I am the Son of God…
- Doing the works of My Father…
- The Father is in Me and I am in the Father.[112]

In case there is any question as to how Jesus' words were received, "The Jews picked up stones again to stone him" not

---

112   John 10:22-38. Notice all the time that Jesus refers to Himself by relationship to the Father, including how now one will snatch out of Jesus' hand those who the Father gave Him for they are likewise in the Father's hand.

for His works "but for blasphemy, because you, being a man, *make yourself God.*"[113]

Jesus is making bold claims, and blindly accepting a claim just because someone makes it would be naïve—you'd risk being seen as gullible and easily deceived. So, what does Jesus do? He invites them to weigh His words in consideration of His works. In effect He says, "I know that what I am saying is hard to swallow. Don't just take My word for it. My works bear witness to Who I am."

Your works speak to who you are. When getting to know someone, what is the next question you typically ask after their name? What do you do? My earliest nickname, that I can remember, was "Dan the Man." Perhaps I acquired it from my excellence in sports, my aptitude for academics, or simply the fact that it rhymes; I don't remember. But then I acquired the nickname, "Dan, Dan, the Scripture man." This was not because I boasted of any scriptural knowledge, but simply because I was constantly sharing Scripture: from the pulpit, in the Bible study, by the hospital bed, in the nursing home, in counseling, in pastoral care... I had a Scripture to share. That nickname evolved into "Dan, Dan, the Preacher Man." Some of my church members are likely thinking, "I get that one. Give the man a pulpit and he becomes the Energizer Bunny: he keeps going, and going, and going, and going, and going, and going.... Then there came, "You are going to be known as the Burying Preacher," due to the large number of funerals that I did serving my first churches.

What I have never, ever been called is, "Dan, Dan, the handyman." I have never been accused of being a "jack of all trades", though master of none perhaps. Why? Because it doesn't fit with who I am. What you do speaks to who you are.

---

113   John 10:31, 33.

Your actions put your character on display. How do you know someone is generous or stingy, kind or mean, dedicated or lazy? It is not through what they say but how they live.

What did Jesus' life say of Him?

> The historian Philip Schaff (in *The Person of Christ*, American Tract Society, 1913) classically describes the uniqueness of the Savior: 'This Jesus of Nazareth, without money and arms, conquered more millions than Alexander, Caesar, Mohammed, and Napoleon; without science and learning, He shed more light on things human and divine than all philosophers and scholars combined; without the eloquence of schools, He spoke such words of life as were never spoken before or since, and produced effects which lie beyond the reach of orator or poet; without writing a single line, He set more pens in motion, and furnished themes for more sermons, orations, discussions, learned volumes, works of art, and songs of praise than the whole army of great men of ancient and modern times.'[114]

How do you understand the extraordinary, dare I say, miraculous, impact Jesus made on the world through His life?

---

114   McDowell, J. (2006). *Evidence for Christianity* (pp. 350–351). Thomas Nelson Publishers.

SHOW AND TELL

When I was in school, we had a time called, "show and tell." You were invited to bring an object to school to show and talk about. The Jews were gathering around Jesus and asking how long He would keep them in suspense. If He were the Christ, they wanted Him to tell them plainly. His answer. I haven't just told you—I've shown you through My works.[115] His works bore witness to Who He was. A big walk backed up His big talk.

Your life either validates or invalidates who you say you are. For instance, I can say that my wife's medical appointments are a priority for me. However, it is only how many appointments I attend, in comparison to how many I miss, that reveals whether it is truly a priority. I can say all sorts of things about myself, nonetheless, what I say is evaluated by what I do.

Jesus made some radical claims; did His life and works support His claims? Amongst the many extraordinary works that Jesus performed, Joe Amaral wrote in *Understanding Jesus: Cultural Insights into the Words and Deeds of Christ*, that there were four specific miracles that Jesus performed that it was believed only the Messiah would be able to do:

- Healing a leper, as leprosy was viewed as a curse by God.
- The exorcism of a demon from a deaf and mute man, as they would be unable to get the demon to identify itself.
- Healing a man who was born blind.
- Raising someone from the dead after four days. It was believed that the spirit lingered for three days.

---

115   John 10:24-25

Guess Who did all those things? If you answered Jesus, then you would be right.

I should point out that while you have reason to believe the Scriptures (see Chapter 3), it is not only the Scriptures that tell you that Jesus performed miracles. Historians such as Josephus record that Jesus performed wondrous works. For all the attacks that came against Jesus, His enemies never denied His accomplishing the miraculous. Rather, they accused Him of where the source of His power came.[116] However, to *suggest* the source of His power as coming from the evil one does not align with His good works, compassion, love, and grace that He continually extended to others. Nor does it account for the wisdom of His teaching recognized by Christians and non-Christians alike.

GET UP AND WALK

In Mark 2:1-12 four friends brought a paralytic to Jesus. They had problems getting to Jesus and so went to the roof, dug a hole, and lowered their friend to Him. Upon Jesus seeing their faith, "he said to the paralytic, 'Son, your sins are forgiven.'"[117] I don't know about you, but I am expecting a healing. The teachers of the law accuse Jesus of blasphemy because God alone can forgive sins. Who does this Jesus think He is to do what only God alone can do? How can you verify whether Jesus *really* has the authority to forgive sins?

> And immediately Jesus, perceiving in his
> spirit that they thus questioned within themselves,
> said to them, "Why do you question these things
> in your hearts? ⁹ Which is easier, to say to the

---

116   See Matthew 9:34, 12:24, for instance.
117   Mark 2:5.

paralytic, 'Your sins are forgiven,' or to say, 'Rise, take up your bed and walk'? [10] But that you may know that the Son of Man has authority on earth to forgive sins"—he said to the paralytic— [11] "I say to you, rise, pick up your bed, and go home." [12] And he rose and immediately picked up his bed and went out before them all, so that they were all amazed and glorified God, saying, 'We never saw anything like this!'[118]

Which is easier to say? Honestly, it is just as easy to say, "get up and walk" as it is to say, "your sins are forgiven." The difference is that you can verify that the man got up and walked. Jesus does what can be seen to ensure His authority to do what cannot be seen. Best show and tell time ever, especially for the man who got up and walked.

A HOUSE DIVIDED OR A KINGDOM COME?

Jesus' enemies never denied the miracles that everyone could see. Rather, they sought to attack His character as one who leads astray or was empowered by Satan. Incidentally, Christian theology does not deny the possibility of counterfeit miracles but informs you to test every spirit and discern based on the kind of fruit produced. "If I am not doing the works of my Father, then do not believe me; [38] but if I do them, even though you do not believe me, believe the works, that you may know and understand that the Father is in me and I am in the Father."[119] Jesus invited His opponents to examine His

---

118   Mark 2:8–12.
119   John 10:37–38.

life for He had nothing to hide. His works verified His words, the man matched the message.

Jesus' life refuted His enemies' allegations. When you pair His actions with His teachings and His life with His message, it becomes clear that His only motive was to glorify the Father. Jesus exposed the flaw in their reasoning as He made His case.

> Knowing their thoughts, he said to them, "Every kingdom divided against itself is laid waste, and no city or house divided against itself will stand. [26] And if Satan casts out Satan, he is divided against himself. How then will his kingdom stand? [27] And if I cast out demons by Beelzebul, by whom do your sons cast them out? Therefore they will be your judges. [28] But if it is by the Spirit of God that I cast out demons, then the kingdom of God has come upon you."[120]

EXAMINE THE WORKS

If there are contradicting opinions, how do you know which is true? You examine and evaluate based on the evidence. Jesus' life was all about giving life. Jesus didn't just preach, "love your enemy," He loved His enemy, even to the point of healing the ear of Malchus when they came to arrest Him[121] and praying for forgiveness for those who crucified Him.[122] The Jews did not pick up stones to stone Jesus for something He had done, but because they were offended by what He said, for what He

---

120   Matthew 12:25–28.
121   Luke 22:51, John 18:10-11.
122   Luke 23:33-34.

said was making Himself out to be God.[123] Of course, it would be blasphemy if it were untrue.

Jesus never said, "Just take my word for it;" He invites us to examine the evidence of His works. Evaluate Jesus by what He did and be honest with the evidence. Examine the impact of His life, miracles, and teachings.

> The famous essay "One Solitary Life" summarizes Jesus' life and impact: 'Here is a man who was born in an obscure village, the child of a peasant woman. He grew up in another village. He worked in a carpenter shop until He was thirty, and then for three years He was an itinerant preacher. He never owned a home. He never wrote a book. He never held an office. He never had a family. He never went to college. He never put his foot inside a big city. He never traveled two hundred miles from the place where He was born. He never did one of the things that usually accompany greatness. He had no credentials but Himself.... While still a young man, the tide of popular opinion turned against Him. His friends ran away. One of them denied Him. He was turned over to His enemies. He went through the mockery of a trial. He was nailed upon a cross between two thieves. While He was dying His executioners gambled for the only piece of property He had on earth—his coat. When He was dead, He was taken down and laid in a borrowed grave through the pity of a friend.

---

123   John 10:33.

Nineteen long centuries have come and gone, and today He is the centerpiece of the human race and the leader of the column of progress. I am far within the mark when I say that all the armies that ever marched, all the navies that ever were built, all the parliaments that ever sat and all the kings that ever reigned, put together, have not affected the life of man upon this earth as powerfully as has that one solitary life.'[124]

Add to the impact of His life the fulfillment of prophecy (chapter 8), the reasons to believe the resurrection (chapter 5), and the case for why Jesus should be case closed.

THE FINAL EXAM

Jesus made one assertion that serves as the final exam for everything else He said and did: that He would die and rise again. The resurrection alone is the one sign or miracle that should make *"why Jesus?"* an open and shut case. Above all, Jesus taught that He must suffer, die, and rise again. If Jesus didn't rise, case closed, no Jesus. However, if He did rise, and you have reason to believe He did (chapter 5), the case is open and shut for Him and awaiting your response.

William Lyon Phelps, for more than forty years Yale's distinguished professor of English literature, and author of some twenty volumes of literary studies, says:

'In the whole story of Jesus Christ, the most important event is the resurrection. Christian

---

124   McDowell, J. (2006). *Evidence for Christianity* (p. 431). Thomas Nelson Publishers.

faith depends on this. It is encouraging to know that it is explicitly given by all four evangelists and told also by Paul. The names of those who saw Him after His triumph over death are recorded; and it may be said that the historical evidence for the resurrection is stronger than for any other miracle anywhere narrated; for as Paul said, if Christ is not risen from the dead then is our preaching in vain, and your faith is also vain. (Phelps, as cited in Smith, GCWC, 18)'[125]

No other religious leader validated His truth claims in such an undeniable and remarkable way as to leave behind an empty tomb. All the other founders of religions are dead. The resurrection was the ultimate proof of Jesus' claims—the defining test that would either confirm or disprove everything He said.

Why Jesus, in a world that offers so many different alternatives? His resurrection, claims, and life together should make an open and shut case, but fulfilled prophecy adds one more element worthy of your consideration.

---

125   McDowell, J. (2006). _Evidence for Christianity_ (p. 261). Thomas Nelson Publishers.

Chapter 8

Fulfilled Prophecy

Luke 24:13-49

FOR OUR SPORTS ENTHUSIASTS

Sports enthusiasts, help me out. How does every football game begin? With the flipping of a coin: heads or tails. Anyone can get lucky and win the coin toss as there is no skill involved, no statistical calculations, and no reading the tea leaves. You have a 50/50 chance.

But what happens when you increase the variables? Rather than calling heads or tails, what about correctly picking the entire NCAA bracket for March Madness? That would be a feat that has never been done perfectly despite millions of brackets being filled out every year. There are too many variables to consider. While educated guesses can be made, surprises cannot be accounted for—such as a team getting hot, going cold, or the injury of a primary player. Inevitably one team overperforms while another underperforms, to the disappointment of all their fans. Great teams are confirmed by their overall record, but even great teams can stumble and fall. Yet there is One who never stumbled, Whose perfect record outshines the rest, and Whose coming and accomplishments were foretold in advance?

PROPHECIES AND PROMISES

I would be remiss to skip over fulfilled prophecy as both a reason to trust the Scriptures and a cause to put your faith in Jesus. While prophecy fascinates some,[126] it is disdained by others. I mean really, how can you tell the future? I can't. I can't raise anyone from the dead either for that matter. Nor can I create something out of nothing. However, God does not suffer from our limitations (chapter 2), and if you accept the reality of God, then not only are miracles possible, but so is prophecy.

By "prophecy," I do not mean predicting events that happen with regularity. Saying, "The sun will rise tomorrow" isn't impressive. I predict I will die. Morbid, maybe, impressive, not. I may make an educated guess about what my wife Amanda may or may not do in a given situation based on history, personality, values, etc., and likely nail it a good percentage of the time, but not perfectly. Past behavior certainly informs expectations but can't account for the occasional surprises.

What about events that do not happen with regularity, or that go contrary to what would have been expected based on experience or educated guesses? How about if I predicted I would die and in three days rise to life? That would be impressive, and certainly not derived from any educated guess or experience, being completely outside the norm. Yet that is

---

126   You might also say it fascinates some too much. You have many prophecy teachers today who have misinterpreted and misapplied Biblical prophecy in attempts to make it fit with today's headlines. When you allow Scripture to interpret Scripture and evaluate prophecy with events that later unfolded in history, the precision of detail and fulfillment is nothing short of miraculous!

what Jesus did. However, if you are still not convinced, let's dive in more deeply into prophecies fulfilled and promises kept, as fulfilled prophecy is a type of miracle that can be tested and verified with the unfolding of history.

HISTORY WRITTEN IN ADVANCE

In Luke 24, Jesus explained to the two men on the road to Emmaus the necessity that the Christ should suffer and die before entering His glory. He did this by walking them through Moses and the prophets. We are not told all the Old Testament Scriptures Jesus referenced, only that He revealed how those Scriptures pertained to Him. To have been a fly on the wall and overhear that conversation would have been amazing.

Anyone can report history. I can tell you exactly what I was doing and where I was when I learned of the horrific 9/11 attacks on the Trade Towers. It was a lived experience for many of you. For others, something that you can learn about through documentaries and books as a matter of historical record.

Likewise, you don't need to read the Bible to know that Jesus was crucified. His execution is a matter of historical record. But the biblical record goes further—it foretells *when* He would come, *when* He would die, and *how* it would happen, centuries in advance. Genesis 49:10[127] was viewed by the Jews as relating to when the Messiah would arrive, Daniel

---

127   The scepter reflected the authority to judge and enforce capital punishment. The Messiah's coming was connected to its departure. Rome removed the scepter around AD 6-7, which is why the Jews took Jesus to Pilate to crucify.

9[128], properly interpreted, gives a timeframe for His death, and Psalm 22 and Isaiah 53 a picture of how He would die hundreds of years before crucifixions occurred. The "…type of death pictured in Isaiah 53 and Psalm 22 did not come into practice under the Jewish system until hundreds of years after the account was written.[129] It has been pointed out a minimum of at least 332 distinct prophecies were fulfilled in Christ relating to His first advent, including His forerunner, His nativity and early years, His mission and office, His passion, His resurrection, and His ascension.[130]

MULTIPLE IMAGES, ONE PICTURE

Since so much had been written of Jesus in advance, you may be wondering: *How did some miss it?* Perhaps you are familiar with those pictures that have embedded multiple images in them. It is typical for someone to have one image pop out while the other remains hidden, that is, until you see it. After you see it, you cannot unsee it. This was the way it was with many Old Testament prophecies. There were multiple images of the Messiah, some of which remained hidden until they finally

---

128   Daniel's 70 weeks is one of the most precise predictions in Scripture, when properly understood. The translation is literally "seventy sevens" and the consensus of scholars is that it refers to units of seven years making 490 years in total. Some schools interpret a gap between the 69th and 70th week interpreting that we still await the 70th week; however, without inserting that gap the timing of this prophecy falls right in line with the crucifixion of Jesus, the anointed One who is cut off putting an end to sacrifice and offering. The scope of these arguments is well beyond what I can put into this book. If you want to dive in more deeply, check out Last Days Madness: Obsession of the Modern Church by Gary DeMar. Disclaimer: when I recommend a book that means that I believe it is worth reading and that there is majority agreement, but not necessarily 100% agreement.

129   McDowell, J. (2006). *Evidence for Christianity* (p. 223). Thomas Nelson Publishers.

130   Check out Josh McDowell's *Evidence that Demands a Verdict*.

saw it. Once seen, you can see how all these images created a composite picture.

Luke 24 brings you to a scene following Jesus' death and reported resurrection. However, as you would expect, the disciples were struggling to believe. It's not every day that someone walks out of the grave. Notice that they are downcast and confused because they *had hoped* Jesus was the One to redeem Israel. They did not believe the reports that He had risen. Interestingly, we are told that they were prevented from recognizing Jesus, but for what purpose?

When I served at Colfax and Arrowsmith Christian churches, I spent one summer surveying the community in Arrowsmith. I recall knocking on one door to be greeted with, "Oh, you're the new pastor living in Colfax." I didn't need her to tell me that, I already knew. But then she said, "You are the one everyone is talking about." This piqued my interest and

I replied, "Tell me more." My family was the talk of the town, and I wanted to know what "everyone" was saying.

Nobody needed to fill Jesus in on the details. He knew better than anyone; however, He invited them to give their interpretation of all that took place. A *suffering, crucified* Messiah was a *stumbling* block to the Jews. They were looking for a conquering King to deliver them from their oppressors, not a suffering servant Who would deliver them from their sins. Both images were and are present in the Old Testament, they had seen the one, but until Jesus explained it, they could not see the other. Once seen, however, it cannot be unseen.

I OBJECT: ALTERED TO FIT

Some raise objections to fulfilled prophecies, arguing that the Gospels were altered to fit them. I dealt with the historical accuracy and trustworthiness of the Bible in chapter 3. I cannot rehash all those arguments here. Suffice it to say, the Bible is not only the best attested historical document we have but there was no motive. The first disciples had nothing to gain by inventing a story but had everything to lose. Most of the first disciples died excruciatingly defending the gospel and following and worshiping Jesus.

Likewise, they didn't do a good job if they had altered the gospels to fit prophecies. They could have been less cryptic in parts and more flattering in others. Repeatedly, the disciples didn't get it, lacking understanding and faith. They were confused, they needed correction, and they were rebuked. If they were to alter the gospel, they would have downplayed the crucifixion rather than emphasizing it. Yet, a disproportionate amount of the gospels is dedicated to the suffering, death, and resurrection of Jesus. The biographies found in Matthew, Mark, Luke, and John were not altered to fit, but to shed light on what was previously misunderstood.

I OBJECT: THE BUCKET LIST

Another objection is not that the gospels were altered to fit prophecy but that knowing prophecies, Jesus intentionally fulfilled them. Jesus, here is the bucket list. However, it doesn't take much to overrule this objection. Do you know who Dan has control over? Dan. And, honestly, sometimes that is questionable. I can choose how I relate to you, but I have no control over how you respond to me, nor do I have control over all my circumstances, don't I wish.

While it is true that Jesus could read about the prophecy of riding into Jerusalem on a donkey and choose to fulfill that prophecy, He had no control over numerous prophecies such as the place of His birth, the time of His birth, His lineage, the amount paid for His betrayal, that He would be handed over to Rome, how He would die, that not a bone would be broken, a spear piercing His side, etc.

For that matter, who would put crucifixion on their bucket list in the first place? The Jews were quick to cling to the prophecies about the Messiah coming in glory while discarding those relating to His suffering and death. Remember, a single picture can contain multiple images—one person may see one image while missing another, even though together they form a unified portrait. Both coming in glory and suffering and dying[131] were present in the Old Testament prophecies. "And [Jesus] said to them, "O foolish ones, and slow of heart to believe all that the prophets have spoken![132] Emphasis on the "all." You need to check this objection off the list. It cannot hold up to numerous fulfilled prophecies pointing to His suffering and death as a prelude to His glory.

I OBJECT: IT'S JUST A COINCIDENCE

Some allege that the New Testament authors misapplied the Old Testament text to force a match. That wouldn't explain belief in the resurrection, the birth of the church, nor those who continue to come to faith in Jesus through studying the Old Testament prophecies. It is true that at times Scripture can be and is taken out of context, but once you understand the cultural context and how the Hebrews understood

---

131   Check out Isaiah 52:13-53:12, for instance.
132   Luke 24:25.

Scripture and how prophecy worked both in direct statements, multilayered meanings, typology, and foreshadowing, such as how the Passover Lamb for Exodus foreshadowed Jesus as our Passover Lamb,[133] you are left with amazing details precisely aligning with Jesus.

It's just a coincidence. Years ago, we were returning from a conference in Texas to our home in Illinois. We happened to stop at a gas station in Missouri, when, after refueling the car, I sought to refuel myself. I was looking for a candy bar and heard someone call out, "Jassman." Some friends from Washburn, Illinois were traveling to Branson, Missouri, and happened to stop at the same gas station in the middle of Missouri at the same time. Most of us would chalk that up as a coincidence. Does the fact that it is now an illustration make it providence?

Despite the odds of us ending up at the same gas station simultaneously, that could be a coincidence. As unlikely as it was, it happened once. However, what if it happened regularly? What if this scene replayed itself repeatedly with various travels, in different states, at diverse times? At what point does that coincidence become, "Stop stalking me?"

At what point does coincidence become providence? Isaiah revealed the manner of the Messiah's birth, of a virgin. Micah disclosed the place of His birth, in Bethlehem. Various passages specify His ancestry, leading Matthew and Luke to include those exciting genealogies. The Psalms foretold His betrayal, accusation by false witnesses, and the manner of His death, even though crucifixion had not yet been invented, as well as how His body would not undergo decay. It has been estimated that Jesus fulfilled around thirty prophecies on the day of His crucifixion alone.

---

133   See John 1:29-36, 1 Corinthians 5:7, 1 Peter 1:17-21, and Revelation 5, for instance.

The more variables and prophecies are layered upon one another, the more unlikely one can argue for coincidence. At what point does it take more faith to believe it was all coincidences rather than providence fulfilling prophecy? Let's turn to the field of science.

> Peter Stoner, a notable figure in the field of probability and prophecy, applied mathematical principles to biblical prophecies in his book "Science Speaks". Stoner analyzed eight prophecies regarding Christ and calculated the probability of all eight being fulfilled by one person as 1 in 100,000,000,000,000,000 (one hundred quadrillion). To illustrate this astronomical odds, he used an analogy involving silver dollars covering the state of Texas two feet deep, with only one marked dollar that a blindfolded person would need to find. Stoner concluded that this demonstrates the improbability of prophets writing these prophecies and having them all come true in any one individual, if they were writing based solely on their own wisdom.[134]

If that is not amazing enough, Stoner considers 48 prophecies and reports all of them being fulfilled in one man as 1 in 10^{157}.[135] The science of probability is beyond my pay grade, but somewhere I believe you left coincidence behind.

---

134   Galaxie Software. (2002). *10,000 Sermon Illustrations*. Biblical Studies Press.

135   Stoner, Peter. *Science Speaks*. https://archive.org/details/sciencespeaks-peterw.stoner.

Jesus asked Cleopas and the other disciples "what things" had been taking place.[136] Jesus then reveals the significance of those events by unfolding the Old Testament Scriptures before them.

> And he said to them, "O foolish ones, and slow of heart to believe all that the prophets have spoken! [26] Was it not necessary that the Christ should suffer these things and enter into his glory?" [27] And beginning with Moses and all the Prophets, he interpreted to them in all the Scriptures the things concerning himself.[137]

Coincidence is overruled by the preponderance of prophecy that finds fulfillment in Jesus.

I OBJECT: IT'S BEEN REDATED

Critics of fulfilled prophecy sometimes attempt to redate large portions of Scripture to avoid the prophetic element. After all, how can someone predict the future? What is impossible with man is possible with God. This is why I already articulated in part one, "The Foundations for the Reasonableness of Faith," the reasons for believing in God, which is further strengthened by fulfilled prophecy. You must guard against starting with a presupposition that refuses to recognize anything that refutes it.

Even if you go with redating much of the Old Testament Scripture to get around the fulfillment of some prophecies that were given with great precision, you cannot get around them all. The Septuagint, the Greek translation of the Old

---

136   Luke 24:17-20.
137   Luke 24:25–27.

Testament, was written around 250 BC. For a translation to exist, the original documents must have already been in place. However liberal your dating methods may be, you are still left with a significant gap of time between the Old Testament prophecies of Jesus and their amazing fulfillment in Jesus.

You likely know people who say they are going to do something, and you think, "I like you, but I will believe it when I see it." When others say something, you might consider it as good as done. What is the difference? Their track record. In a world with so many alternatives, why Jesus? His resurrection, His claims, His life, and the fulfillment of prophecy are all building a case for Jesus. May it not be said of you, "O foolish ones, and slow of heart to believe",[138] but rather given Jesus' powerful track record that you are beginning to see how Jesus is unlike any other leader, truly in a field of His own.

---

138   Luke 24:25-26.

Chapter 9

In A Field of His Own

Mark 6:1-6

Throughout school, I participated in many sports. I played baseball, volleyball, golf, and basketball, ran track, and cross country. I was competitive but far from the best in any of them. However, I recall one year at the state track meet when a sprinter dominated his field. I do not recall his name, but I remember him running the 200 meters and looking behind him. He was smiling because there was nobody remotely near him. When there is an athlete of such caliber, you might say that they are in a field of their own.

Whether in sports, medicine, teaching, or any other field, there are always those who seem to excel above the rest. Their impact on the field is unparalleled as people recognize their achievements. However, the stars come and go. Often replaced by new rising stars. The greats are eventually replaced, and the world moves on. Has there ever been somebody who was truly irreplaceable?

THE INTERVIEW

Many of you have experienced going through an interview process. An interview is one of the rare occasions when you are expected to promote yourself as the best candidate for a position. The goal is to set yourself apart from the competition in some way as the best candidate for the position, whatever it may be. Others may be just as qualified—perhaps even more so—though in that interview, you certainly hope not. In most cases, someone held the position before you, and someone will hold it after you. With or without you, the role will be filled.

Similarly, all the religions of the world, except Christianity, could exist without their religious founders. This is not to diminish who those founders were nor what they achieved, only that someone else could have delivered the same teachings and provided us with that religious system. In contrast, if you remove Jesus from Christianity, Christianity crumbles. Every other religion could have someone else fill the shoes of its founder, but not Christianity, which depends as much on Who Jesus is as it does what Jesus taught and did.

Tal Davis wrote,

> Christianity does not stand or fall on its moral principles or depth of mystical experience. If that were true, then it would be no better than any other religion of the world, and Jesus Christ would be only another great religious or moral teacher. No, Christianity stands or falls entirely on the person and work of one man: Jesus Christ. Either he was who he claimed to be, the Lord of the universe, who came to earth as a man, lived a sinless life, died on the cross as an atonement

for our sins, and rose again from the dead, or the entire Christian faith is a gigantic lie.[139]

As Paul put it, "And if Christ has not been raised, your faith is futile and you are still in your sins.[140] He didn't say that faith hinges on Jesus' teachings or morality, but on the resurrection, which also demonstrated that Jesus was and is the Son of God.[141] It was only because of Who Jesus is that He could die in your place for your sins.

But why? As I shared earlier from Ravi Zacharias,

> In every other religion, there is a distinction between the person and the teaching. It is not Zoroaster to whom you turn. It is Zoroaster to whom you listen. It is not Buddha who delivers you; it is his Noble Truths that instruct you. It is not Mohammad who transforms you; it is the beauty of the Koran that woos you. By contrast, Jesus did not only teach or expound His message. He was identical with His message. 'In Him,' say the Scriptures, 'dwelt the fullness of the Godhead bodily.' He did not just proclaim the truth. He said, 'I am the truth.' He did not just show the way. He said, 'I am the way.' He did not just open vistas. He said, 'I am the door.' 'I am the Good

---

139   Davis, Tal. *Evidence for God: 50 Arguments for Faith from the Bible, History, Philosophy, and Science.* Ed by William A. Dembski and Michael R. Licona. Grand Rapids, Michigan: Baker Books, 2010, p188.

140   1 Corinthians 15:17.

141   See Romans 1:4.

Shepherd.' 'I am the resurrection and the life.' 'I am the I AM'.[142]

Jesus came as a savior to deliver not simply as a teacher to be followed. Every other religion is about what you do to reach God, gods, or some path, Christianity is about what God has done to reach you and save you. The difference being between what you do and what God has done.

As you "interview" the leaders whom you may or may not choose to follow, recall what you learned from the 'minimal facts,' those facts accepted even by the most liberal scholars, that even with a very stringent filter Jesus deemed Himself greater than any previous or future religious figure. He believed He possessed the authority of God, could forgive sins, would judge the world at the end of history, and even received worship. It is not rude to compare candidates for a job interview, so why should you think it rude to compare and contrast religious leaders and their teachings? Groothuis comments: "In a religiously pluralistic setting, it is not rude or imperious to compare and contrast the teachings of religions and their leaders; it is apologetically necessary."[143]

If you pictured all the different religious founders as candidates interviewing for the position of your religious leader, wouldn't you want the best, one who stood in a field of His own? Along with His resurrection, His claims, His life, and fulfilled prophecy, one more item to add to His resume is that He is truly in a field of His own; He is unlike any other leader. Jesus stands out and stands above the rest.

---

142   Zacharias, Ravi. *Jesus Among Other Gods: The Absolute Claims of the Christian Message*. Nashville, Tennessee: Word Publishing, 2000, p89. Zoroaster was an ancient Iranian prophet who founded. Zoroastrianism.
143   Groothuis, Douglas. *Christian Apologetics: A Comprehensive Case for Biblical Faith*. Downers Grove, IL: Intervarsity Press, 2011, p. 500.

In a sense, asking how Jesus differs from other religious leaders is like asking how the sun differs from other stars in our solar system—the point being that there are no other stars in our solar system! No other 'religious leader' can compare to Jesus Christ. Every other religious leader is either alive or dead. Jesus Christ is the only one who was dead and is now alive.[144]

REFERENCES

Some people think highly of me—I'm not sure why, but they do. Then there are those who truly know me. I say this with a bit of humor, but we've all encountered people we thought we knew, only to realize later that we didn't know them as well as we believed. I've had experiences where people have come to me and asked if I would be a reference for them for a job. I expect they thought it would be good to have a pastor as a reference, and often, without references, you are not likely to even get your interview. The problem was, I didn't know them that well. Sure, I knew who they were, but since they only attended church on Christmas and Easter and I never saw them otherwise, I could not say I truly knew them. At least not well enough to give a reference.

Remember young love? That must be where they came up with the saying, "Love is blind." It is amazing the personality quirks that you can overlook and the things that you don't see initially. Marriage restores that sight. As you do life together, you learn who someone is. The best references for Jesus were the disciples who did life with Him.

---

144   https://www.gotquestions.org/Jesus-different.html

The rabbi-disciple relationship was not, see you every Sabbath when I hear a message, then walk out with a "Good sermon, Rabbi, see you next week." It required doing life together. Whether early morning, high noon, or late night: together. They walked with Jesus daily for roughly three and half years, witnessing how He ministered, listening to what He taught, and watching how He interacted with friend and foe alike. You have already looked at what Jesus claimed of Himself, call it His interview, if you will (chapter 6). What did His references have to say?

While Jesus was at times called a blasphemer, out of his mind and even demon possessed …, he and others made some remarkable claims about his moral character. Pontius Pilate found no basis for convicting him as a criminal (Luke 23:4). A centurion who witnessed his death on the cross said, 'Surely this was a righteous man' (Luke 23:47). The criminal crucified next to Jesus declared, 'This man has done nothing wrong' (Luke 23:41). [Okay, okay, okay. But what about those closest to Him, what did they say?] The testimony of his disciples is telling. John refers to him as 'full of grace and truth' (John 1:14) and as 'Jesus Christ, the Righteous One' (1 John 2:1) in whom there is no sin (1 John 3:5). Peter praised Jesus as 'a lamb without blemish or defect' (1 Peter 1:19) who never spoke deceitfully (1 Peter 2:22). Paul confessed that Jesus 'had no sin' as the spotless sacrifice for sinners (2 Corinthians 5:21). Even Judas confessed, 'I have betrayed innocent blood' (Matthew 27:4). Hebrews speaks of the greatness of Jesus as the perfect high priest 'who was tempted in every way, just as we are—yet he did not sin (Hebrews 4:15; see also Hebrews 7:26-28).[145]

The same certainly could not be said of me, or any other religious leader throughout history. In no other religion do the followers claim their founders to have been perfect and/or without sin. Abraham was renowned for his faith, yet you read in the Bible his failures of faith. The beloved King David, a man after God's heart, was a man who occasionally desperately fell apart. The pivotal leader Peter had to learn how to self-lead as he was continually blundering and sticking his foot in his mouth. The Scriptures readily reveal the faults and failings of all the heroes, except Jesus, to Whom was reported, was "... tempted as we are, yet without sin.[146]

WORK EXPERIENCE

Don't you love the part of the interview when you are asked, "Tell me about your strengths and weaknesses?" Jesus had no weaknesses to speak of, and His work experience, well, you might say that it was nothing short of miraculous.

The profound and powerful life of Jesus as a historical figure has made a dramatic impact on the rest of history. Noted Yale historian Jaroslav Pelikan writes, 'Regardless what anyone may personally think or believe about him, Jesus of Nazareth has been the dominant figure in the

145   Groothuis, Douglas. *Christian Apologetics: A Comprehensive Case for Biblical Faith*. Downers Grove, IL: Intervarsity Press, 2011, p493.
146   Hebrews 4:15.

history of Western culture for almost twenty centuries. If it were possible, with some sort of supermagnet to pull up out of that history every scrap of metal bearing at least a trace of his name, how much would be left?' (Pelikan, JTC, 1). His impact on the course of history is without parallel.[147]

Jeremiah Johnston wrote an excellent book called, *Unimaginable: What Our World Would Be Like without Christianity*, where he lays out the impact of those influenced by the teachings of Jesus. From advancements in social justice to the rise of education and science, to the building of hospitals, as well as intellectual advancements and recognizing the dignity of humanity, you cannot overestimate the impact and influence of Jesus on the world. Jesus is the most influential life ever lived, and uniquely, it was His death that gave His life such power and grew His influence over those who would follow Him. Even other religious traditions, though they differ in their understanding of Jesus' identity, are compelled to address the life of One Who redefined history.

PERSONAL BRAND

"And on the Sabbath he began to teach in the synagogue, and many who heard him were astonished, saying, "Where did this man get these things? What is the wisdom given to him? How are such mighty works done by his hands?"[148] Mighty works done by His hand certainly seem to reflect great work experience as the crowds recognized His wisdom and power.

---

147   McDowell, J. (2006). *Evidence for Christianity* (p. 192). Thomas Nelson Publishers.
148   Mark 6:2.

Whether or not you believe in the possibility of miracles, history attests that Jesus performed them. Physical evidence in antiquity reveals Jews and pagans alike invoking the name of Jesus for healing. A documentary called, "Fragments of Truth" includes an archeological discovery of a cup with a reference to Jesus as a wondrous healer and an incantation from a pagan exorcist referencing "the power of Jesus, the God of the Hebrews." Whether you accept miracles or reject them, the evidence of history, from the Biblical record along with Roman and Jewish historians, understood Jesus to be a miracle worker.

So, His work experience is looking pretty impressive. Everybody loves to experience a miracle, but let's be honest. Miracles impacted individual lives while Jesus' words would go on to change the world. Sample interview questions may be, "How do you handle difficult people?" Jesus taught you to love and pray for even your enemies, which He likewise modeled for you. "How did you handle a tough situation?" "Well, there was this time that I died, then I rose again."

The resurrection alone sets Jesus apart, but when combined with His teaching that He died for your sins (and let's be honest, you and I are those difficult people), it becomes even more profound. Unlike any other religion, Jesus offers something unique—true assurance of forgiveness through His sacrifice. Your forgiveness is no longer based on being good enough or doing enough for He did, and He is, if you just put your faith in Him and the grace He offers to you.

BACKGROUND CHECK

How can Jesus deliver on what no other spiritual leader can? You are back to Who Jesus is, or His background. "Is not this the carpenter, the son of Mary and brother of James and Joses and Judas and Simon? And are not his sisters here with us?" And they took offense at him."[149] You would find nothing offensive in being a carpenter, yet in this context it is not a compliment. They could not understand how a carpenter had such wisdom, authority, and power in His teaching?

You have heard of hometown pride. Sometimes it works the other way. "And Jesus said to them, "A prophet is not without honor, except in his hometown and among his relatives and in his own household."[150] They knew Jesus as a carpenter and had difficulty accepting Him as a master Rabbi, or more. They could not wrap their minds around the boy who grew up down the street possibly being the Messiah they had waited centuries for. Rather they reasoned, "Is this not...the son of Mary"? This question may not mean much to you in our culture, but this stands out in a culture where a person is associated with their father. This question may be a reaction to Jesus' followers teaching the "virgin birth," as the virgin conceiving and giving birth was the teaching of the early church.

You may say, "I can't believe in a virgin birth." Or, you might think, "What does it matter?" The virgin conception and birth are the necessary background qualifying Jesus to be able to die for your sins. Jesus had to come in the flesh to identify with sinful humanity but also had to be more than a mere man to be free from the nature of sin. The Son of God became the son of man so that the sons and daughters of men

---

149   Mark 6:3.
150   Mark 6:4.

might become children of God. The God who created the world would certainly have no issue with creating a life outside the normal means.

With that said, some argue that the virgin birth was taken or copied from pagan religions. If you investigate the pagan religions, there was nothing "virgin" about them. Nothing else in the ancient world reflects the simplicity of the Biblical account and there are no explanations for the origin of the virgin birth outside of the early witness of the church. While the virgin birth cannot be proven historically in the same way that you can examine the resurrection and the reality of God, it is plausible when you consider the reality of God, the evidence for the resurrection, and the impact of Jesus on the world stage.

MAKING THE HIRE

Once you examine the evidence, or interview the candidates, you realize that faith in Jesus is not a blind leap, but a reasonable step. He is unlike any other, truly in a field of His own. So why would some take offense at Him? Though an interview is designed to highlight the best candidate, that is not always the case. Judgment can be clouded, preferences or politics come into play, relationships a factor. At times, the best person doesn't get the position.

You seldom read of Jesus being amazed. However, you do read that He marveled both at the faith He found outside of Israel[151] and the unbelief within.[152] Too many were blinded by preconceived prejudices to really see and so dismissed Him as less than He was. They couldn't see beyond a carpenter, Mary's son. They were astonished at His wisdom and His mighty

---

151 Matthew 8:10.
152 Mark 6:6.

works, yet managed to rationalize it away. They missed Who was before their eyes and consequently failed to receive the One Whom they had been waiting for. They failed to realize that Jesus was not only the One Whom they had been waiting for, but He was much more as you will explore in chapter 10.

The Trinity

Romans 1:1-7

JUST BECAUSE IT DOESN'T MAKE SENSE TO YOU, DOESN'T MEAN IT'S UNTRUE

Amanda had thyroid cancer in 2001, which was a catalyst for not feeling well for years. Everything went smoothly with her cancer surgery and treatment, and thankfully, she has remained cancer-free. However, after her treatment, there were simply no answers as to why she didn't feel well. She would go to one doctor who would say from their end that everything looked fine and be sent to another doctor, only to repeat the cycle with no answers.

Eventually, this led us to a clinic up north that was more homeopathic and utilized what I believe was called kinesiology and muscle testing as an aid for diagnosing. They would have her hold out her arm, touch some point on her body, and test her strength. Whatever happened to good old-fashioned blood work or peeing in a cup?

If the whole idea sounds weird to you, I'll admit, this was one of those times that I had a thought and couldn't believe that

I said it out loud. I told the doctor, "You've got to be kidding me," and laughed at this method of testing. Surprisingly, this clinic made a diagnosis that had eluded all of Amanda's other doctors for seven years. The cancer surgery and radiation had triggered an undiagnosed gluten allergy.

While it is not perfect science, what I had first laughed out, I came to learn had some merit. We found a chiropractor who also employed this muscle testing method, leading to a conclusion later confirmed by bloodwork from a more traditional doctor. Different methods yielded the same result. I understand how bloodwork works, but not so much how muscle testing does.

We laugh, mock, and scoff at what doesn't make sense to us. However, simply because something doesn't make sense *to you* doesn't mean it is untrue. What you may not understand doesn't mean it is not understandable to someone else. Try explaining calculus to a kindergartner. Some of you may be thinking, try explaining calculus to me. Or, how about Einstein's theory of relativity, or gravity. Some truths are undeniable, even if we don't fully understand them. Despite all that science has uncovered about gravity and the universe, much remains beyond our grasp.

A BLURRING OF THE LINES

remember the former things of old; for I am God, and there is no other; I am God, and there is none like me, [10] declaring the end from the beginning and from ancient times things not yet done, saying, 'My counsel shall stand, and I will accomplish all my purpose'.[153]

Isaiah declared that God knows the end from the beginning, which explains the accuracy of prophetic predictions. Nonetheless, that only supports the primary declaration: God is unique and there is only one God.

Judaism, Christianity, and Islam all agree that there is one God Who is unique; their differences are in understanding Who this God is and what His character is like. God's nature is where the New Testament gets radical in understanding the uniqueness and oneness of God as the lines get a little blurry. Paul is a servant of Christ Jesus but has been set apart for the gospel of God. How can he be a servant, or more literally a slave, of One, yet set apart for the Other? For that matter, Paul calls it the gospel of God, yet it is all about Jesus and the gospel of His Son. Jesus is also called Lord and the One to Whom you are called to belong. Why would a lifelong Jew, trained as Paul was, speak of being called to belong to Jesus rather than belonging to God?[154]

Some of you may be into genealogies. When you explore your genealogy, you don't need to point out, "descended from…according to the flesh," as it is a given. Yet, Paul distinguishes between "according to the flesh" and "according to the Spirit," between the human nature, descended from David, and divine nature, declared to be the Son of God. Likewise, God alone is the Holy One, yet you are introduced to the "Spirit of holiness."

---

153   Isaiah 46:9–10.
154   Romans 1:1-9 is only one passage where we see language ascribed to Jesus that was beforehand limited and restricted to God. We also looked at this a bit with the claims of Jesus, where Jesus' enemies understood that He was "making Himself equal with God" (John 5:18).

Are you confused by the blurring of language? Hang in there as I hope to unravel the confusion. First, you need to see the blurring of the lines in how language ascribed to God, Who is one, is likewise attributed to Jesus and the Holy Spirit. For those who like trivia, Who raised Jesus from the dead? God, the Holy Spirit, or Jesus? It was God Who raised this Jesus to life,[155] the Spirit Who raised Jesus from the dead,[156] and Jesus Who took His life up again.[157] Repeatedly you see the blurring of lines with Who is Who and Who does what. Remember that just because something doesn't make sense to you, doesn't make it untrue. However, if you hang with me, I hope to help bring some clarity.

GOD WILL NOT SHARE HIS GLORY WITH ANOTHER

Both the Old Testament and the New Testament declare that God is unique, that there is only one God, and that He will not give His glory to another.[158] Yet, Jesus is given glory and worshipped in the New Testament. While it is true that the Greeks and Romans could conceive of the idea of a god-man, this was not true of the Jews. What happened that thousands of Jews would come to believe that Jesus was God incarnate, or God come in the flesh?

> Paul, a servant of Christ Jesus, called to be an apostle, set apart for the gospel of God, [2] which he promised beforehand through his prophets in the holy Scriptures, [3] concerning his Son, who

---

155   Acts 2:32.
156   Romans 8:11.
157   John 10:17-18.
158   Isaiah 42:8. Yet, notice how God gives glory to Jesus throughout the Gospel of John.

was descended from David according to the
flesh ⁴ and was declared to be the Son of God
in power according to the Spirit of holiness by
his resurrection from the dead, Jesus Christ our
Lord,[159]

What happened? The resurrection.

Paul, who wrote Romans, was a monotheistic Jew, as were
the majority of the first Christians. Nonetheless, the Bible and
extrabiblical sources reveal that along with Gentiles who came
to faith in Jesus were all these monotheistic Jews who oddly
enough began worshipping Jesus, Who had been crucified.
Rather strange to worship a crucified man unless there is more
to the story, such as the resurrection.

Some critics might suggest, "Wait a minute." Paul says,
"Son of God." They may suggest theories such as adoption,
a lesser god, or God playing different roles at different times.
However, the apostle John, who was part of Jesus' inner circle,
refutes those theories as he wrote, "And we know that the Son
of God has come and has given us understanding, so that we
may know him who is true; and we are in him who is true, in
his Son Jesus Christ. He is the true God and eternal life."[160]
Son of God...in His Son...*true God* lays other theories to rest,
as does how the people understood the claims Jesus made of
Himself, accusing Him of making Himself equal with God
and charging Him with blasphemy.[161]

---

159   Romans 1:1–4.
160   1 John 5:20.
161   John 5:18, 10:33. See also Matthew 26:65 and Mark 14:64.

THE DOCTRINE THE WORLD SCOFFS AT

To make things more interesting, it is not just between God and Jesus that the lines are blurred, but also with the Holy Spirit—since lying to the Holy Spirit is equated to lying to God.[162] Welcome to the doctrine that the world scoffs at and that Christians cringe to answer. On the surface it appears contradictory and beyond believability: God is three in one, and one in three, that must be contradictory, can't you see? Or is it?

I don't understand muscle testing. Neither do I comprehend how voices can be carried wirelessly between phones or sounds via radio. I can't figure out how women think. But just because it doesn't make sense to you, doesn't make it untrue.

The doctrine of the Trinity is a teaching that distinguishes Christianity and Jesus from any other religion and is often the target of ridicule. "Irrationality has been the yoke put around the neck of the Incarnation and the Trinity. How can Jesus, at the same time, be both fully God and fully man? How can one God be three persons simultaneously?[163] While the Trinity may be beyond full comprehension, we cannot use that as an excuse to dismiss a doctrine that challenges our understanding. Just because we can't fully grasp it doesn't mean it's contradictory.

People have attempted to describe the Trinity with all sorts of analogies. Cherry pie, one pie cut in three slices is still one pie. Water in three states, solid, liquid, and gas. Or even by the different hats one may wear, I am a husband, father, and grandfather. However, some analogies fall more into tritheism,

---

162   Acts 5:3-4.
163   Merritt, James. *God, I've Got a Question: Biblical Truth for Our Deepest Concerns*. Eugene, Oregon: Harvest House, 2011, p43.

three gods, or modalism, one God Who expressed Himself differently at different times. First as the Father, then as the Son, then as the Holy Spirit.

> In the beginning was the Word, and the Word was with God, and the Word was God. ² He was in the beginning with God.[164] And the Word became flesh and dwelt among us, and we have seen his glory, glory as of the only Son from the Father, full of grace and truth.[165]

The language expresses the idea that somehow the Word was God yet was distinct from the Father, and this Word became flesh. On the one hand, throughout the Gospels you discover that Jesus prays to the Father, reveals the Father, the Father loves the Son, the Son does the will of the Father, up to the cross where Jesus cries out, "My God, my God, why have you forsaken me."[166] These verses indicate a distinction between the Son and the Father. On the other hand, I have already highlighted how Jesus' enemies understood Him to be making Himself "equal to God" by applying language to Himself that was ascribed to God in the Old Testament. Two dangers that you must be careful of are losing the personal differentiation between Father, Son, and Holy Spirit for the sake of one God, or losing one God for the sake of differentiating the Father, Son, and Holy Spirit.

---

164 John 1:1–2.
165 John 1:14.
166 Matthew 27:46.

OLD TESTAMENT CLUES

How can it be both the gospel of God and the gospel of Jesus (Romans 1:1-9)? How can Jesus have both a human nature (1:3) as well as a divine nature (1:4)? How can the Spirit be holy and play a role in the resurrection (1:4), if only God is holy, and God raised Jesus? You have already examined the trustworthiness of Scripture in what can be observed in Chapter 3 to provide the basis for its trustworthiness in what cannot be observed. Does the Old Testament prepare you for the revelation in the New Testament of the unique nature of God—three in one and one in three?

One of the names used for God is Elohim, which is a plural term that grammatically gets paired with singular verbs. "In the beginning, God created the heavens and the earth.[167] What you do not see in the English is that the Hebrew translated God is in the plural while created is in the singular. Similarly in Genesis 1:26-27, the name of God is in the plural and "image" in the singular. Unfortunately, sometimes I suffer from bad grammar. However, it has been pointed out that bad grammar in the Bible equals good theology. The grammar is to catch people's attention in making a statement.[168]

"Hear, O Israel: The Lord our God, the Lord is one[169] is a pivotal verse for the Jews found in Deuteronomy. Lord is a translation of the name of God in the singular. God, however, is the term Elohim, and in the plural. And one, well, one is back to the singular. These passages from the Old Testament are

---

167   Genesis 1:1.
168   I am using a couple of verses from Genesis as an example, but this is not limited to Genesis. There are various times in Revelation that "bad grammar" occurs, which serves as a hint that John is echoing something from the Old Testament that he wants to call the reader's attention to.
169   Deuteronomy 6:4.

far from able to establish the doctrine of the Trinity; however, they lead you toward the doctrine of the Trinity rather than away from it.

HELP FROM SCIENCE

What is concealed in the Old Testament is revealed in the New Testament or at least given greater light. This greater illumination reflects the progressive nature of revelation in the Scripture. But do you have any help in thinking that what may not make sense to you on the surface is anything but nonsense? Could it be that there are not only clues in the Old Testament, but that science can help you make sense of the incarnation: Jesus being both man and God, part of the Trinity? How God can be three in one and one in three? Could it be that in nature God has provided you with clues to help in understanding His nature?

Welcome to the world of waves and particles. How can Jesus be both man and God? How can light be both a wave and a particle? I'll be honest, the science is beyond me. However, in the world of science, scientists have discovered

> A world where, in certain circumstances, light behaves like a wave and in others like a particle. Ditto for an electron; sometimes it behaves like a particle, sometimes a wave. ... What science appears to have discovered is that a light ray and an electron are each *fully* a wave and *fully* a particle. Each is the embodiment of a contradiction.[170]

---

170   Guillen, Dr. Michael. *Amazing Truths: How Science and the Bible Agree.* Grand Rapids, Michigan: Zondervan, 2015, p44.

This scientific discovery reflects what the New Testament teaches regarding the nature of Jesus: *fully* God and *fully* man. Interestingly, Jesus is described as the light of the world.[171] Light functioning as both fully a wave and fully a particle helps shed light on the incarnation: that Jesus can be both fully God and fully man. You may not comprehend how this dual nature works, but science provides a similar situation with waves and particles.

But what about being three in one and one in three? The Trinity appears contradictory. However, appearances can be deceiving. I have heard many illustrations and analogies attempting to explain the Trinity. The best I have heard relates to an organic unity rather than a mathematical unity. Our thinking is 1 + 1 + 1= 3, and mathematically speaking it is. However, is there a different way that you can think about it? Organically, you have an example of 1 + 1 + 1 = 1. Take a substance you have likely heard about called glucose. The chemical formula for glucose is $C_6H_{12}O_6$. Carbon, hydrogen, and Oxygen are all distinct from one another. Just as it's impossible to have glucose without all three elements, the Father, Son, and Holy Spirit are distinct, yet together they form the unified Godhead.

Difficult to comprehend? Absolutely. But why should you expect God to be easily comprehended? The point is not that the Trinity is easy to understand but that the doctrine is not self-contradictory when properly understood, and you even have an example in nature to help you to understand the nature of God: three distinct persons, Father (1), Son (+1), and Holy Spirit (+1), but in essence one Godhead (=1), an organic unity.

---

171   John 1:1-9, 8:12, 9:5.

WHY DOES IT MATTER?

Why Jesus in a world with so many alternatives? Paul recaps in these few verses from Romans a variety of themes we have covered. The resurrection (chapter 5) validates Jesus' claims (chapter 6) and serves as the exclamation point on His life (chapter 7), declaring Him with power to be the Son of God. Jesus was both a descendent of David, according to the flesh, and as a fulfillment of prophecy (chapter 8), but likewise, the Son of God, part of the Trinity, putting Him in a field of His own unlike any other religious founder (chapters 9 and 10).

This topic is heavily theological, so how are you to respond? What is the relevance? Judaism, Christianity, and Islam all teach the concept of one God but very different things about Who God is. What you believe shapes how you behave and who you follow. If there is one God, and He has revealed Himself to you through His Son, Jesus, then it is to Jesus you need to listen and follow.

The politically incorrect reality is that you are not talking about one God among gods or an alternative path among various paths. When different religions teach contradictory doctrines, as they do, they cannot all be true. If Jesus indeed has been raised from the dead and thus declared to be the Son of God in power, and you have a historical, archeological, logical, and even scientific basis for faith in Him, that leaves you with one question: how are you responding to Him?

To call people from all the nations to belong to Him is to call them from other religious or worldly paths and to the obedience of faith in Jesus.[172] Jesus being the only way to the Father is a teaching many people do not like. The question is not, do you like it, but is it true?

---

172   Romans 1:5-6.

Chapter 11

Not Simply Another Option

John 14:1-14

Truth is not determined by what you like or dislike. If only it were! You would never get a bad diagnosis. You would always have money left over at the end of the month. The car would never break down. The house would never need repair. That furnace would never go out on the coldest day of the year, nor would the air conditioning fail on the hottest day. Marriages would never fall apart. People would always be trustworthy. I could go on, but I trust that I have made the point: truth is not determined by what you like or dislike, but (are you ready for this) by what is true.

A QUICK RECAP

In the last chapter, you plunged into the complicated teaching of the Trinity, that God is one in essence, but three in person: Father, Son, and Holy Spirit. John reiterates this thought as you encounter the call to not only trust in God but also in

Jesus,[173] Who is identified with the Father,[174] yet distinct from Him.[175] You examined how the idea of the Trinity is not a contradiction to one God, Who is unique, and distinguishes Christianity from any other religion while simultaneously fitting with the evidence and offering the best explanation for the record of history.

My hope and prayer are that as you have journeyed through philosophy, history, logic, the Scriptures, and even science, if you are a believer, you have been strengthened in your faith and better equipped to share it. If you are on the fence or not a believer, my prayer is that you are beginning to see how Jesus is unique among all the alternatives and worthy of serious consideration. This is especially true as you confront one of the most controversial aspects of Jesus' teaching.

I AM THE WAY, THE TRUTH, AND THE LIFE

You need to first deal with the evidence for Jesus before being confronted with one of the most controversial statements of Jesus. "Jesus said to him, "I am the way, and the truth, and the life. No one comes to the Father except through me."[176] This is a difficult statement for our pluralistic culture, which wants to accept that there are diverse paths leading to God. Ironically, in the name of inclusion and tolerance, the idea of multiple paths seeks to enfold all these different religions but runs counter to what most major religions teach.

Christianity often takes the hit of being labeled exclusivist; however, Judaism, Islam, and, for that matter, any religion you evaluate honestly, exclude many other religions at some

---

173 John 14:1, 12.
174 John 14:7, 9-11.
175 John 14:1, 2, 6, 12.
176 John 14:6.

level. Even the most inclusive religions exclude those they don't deem inclusive enough. How we arrived at a rejection of objective truth attempting to present "all roads lead to God" may be a matter of debate, but Sam Storms offers the following possibilities. An increase in globalization through TV, ease of travel, and the internet has exposed us to far more cultures and beliefs. High levels of immigration have brought ideas that used to be "out there" to our neighborhood. There has been a redefinition of tolerance from not hindering someone to not saying anything that may offend someone.[177] We have elevated sincerity over truth. Never mind that you can be sincere, and sincerely wrong. We have elevated and idolized the idea that whatever works for you is true for you. However, this idea fails to differentiate between that which is preference and that which is objectively true.

Honestly, I find the idea of multiple paths appealing. It would make my job a lot easier. The idea of universal salvation, which I had never heard until seminary, and that everyone is saved is a nice sentiment. It is also a nice thought that people are all good, that there is no corruption in politics, and that decisions are made for the good of the people rather than someone's pocketbook. Nonetheless, just because I want to believe something doesn't make it true. Unfortunately, diverse paths to God are nothing more than a feel-good theology without any foundation and are logically incoherent. If Jesus is the only way, then is it not the most loving thing to tell you so?

---

177   Storms, Sam. *Tough Topics 2: Biblical answers to 25 challenging questions.* Scotland, Great Britain: Christian Focus Publications, 2015, p99-100.

THE NEMESIS OF PLURALISTS

Have you had that lovely experience of having someone ask a question you just answered? "Thomas said to him, "Lord, we do not know where you are going. How can we know the way?"[178] Where is there? Jesus had just told them a couple of verses earlier; that He was going to His Father's House to prepare a place.[179] The way to get somewhere depends on the destination and the starting point. You can't give directions without knowing the destination and the starting point. That is unless you don't care where the destination is, which is not a good plan for eternity.

What is physically true is spiritually relevant. How can you say that all paths lead to God when the various religions teach very different things about God, if they even lead to God, or a god in the first place? Different religions propose different destinations. Buddhism and Hinduism talk of the cessation of the self and the elimination of desire. Islam speaks of a paradise, but not one that has the intimacy and the fellowship with the Father that Jesus taught you about in John. If they present different ideas of where you end up, how can they all be paths to the same destination?

The nemesis of religious pluralism, or the idea that all religions lead to God and/or at their core teach the same thing, is that every religion makes truth claims that contradict other religious truth claims regarding Who God is, our origins, human nature, morality, and ultimately our destiny. These are not superficial matters but fundamental teachings that any religion must address. It would be like saying if I want to go to Chicago I must head north, which is true from where I live,

178   John 14:5.
179   John 14:2.

but I want to head south instead and will somehow still get to Chicago. Ravi Zacharias observed that tolerance has become a euphemism for contradiction; we would rather live with a contradiction than search for truth.[180] However, the denial of truth is ultimately self-defeating. As a British philosopher comments in his critiques on relativism, "A writer who says that there are no truths is asking you not to believe him. So don't."[181]

THE MOST INCLUSIVE EXCLUSIVIST

"Jesus said to him, "I am the way, and the truth, and the life. No one comes to the Father except through me."[182] This is not John's claim, nor my claim, but Jesus' claim. If anyone takes issue with this claim, their issue is with Jesus. This is not a matter of whether you believe Dan, or some celebrity, it is a matter of whether you believe Jesus.

Whether you like or dislike a statement doesn't change its truthfulness. Perhaps you have learned a truth you didn't like. Maybe you've been confronted with the reality that you are getting older, that you cannot eat how you used to, that you overspent on the credit card, or by the test that came back from the doctor. Occasionally the truth is not pretty, and it may be far from your liking, but that doesn't make it untrue. Logically speaking, truth corresponds to reality, and so by definition excludes that which is not true. The best way for me to get to Chicago is not by heading south, and it is not

---

180   Zacharias, Ravi. *Jesus Among Other Gods: The Absolute Claims of the Christian Message.* Nashville, Tennessee: Word Publishing, 2000, 36.

181   I had used in a previous sermon but did not recall where to find the source and so searched for on ChatGPT which attributes the quote to a British philosopher named Roger Scruton.

182   John 14:6.

unloving or exclusive for someone to give the right directions for where I want to go.

People can be sincere—and still be sincerely wrong, a reality we've all faced. Wanting something to be true doesn't make it so. It's not just belief that matters, but what you believe. Jesus calls you not only to trust in God but to place your faith in Him. Why? Faith is only as good as the object or person in which it is placed. I can have strong resolute faith in thin ice, or weak faith in thick ice. Which will hold me? It is not generic faith in anything that saves you, but faith in the One with power to save, Jesus. While that may sound exclusivist, Jesus is very inclusive in that He invites "whoever will" to come.

It has been said that Jesus is the most inclusive exclusivist, as no one who desires to come is denied. It doesn't matter whether you are male or female, young or old, fool or wise, Jew or Gentile; it doesn't matter what nation you come from or what race and ethnicity you may be. It doesn't matter how talented you are or even how good you have been. Jesus says, "come to Me"[183] for as the Way He is the answer to your sin, as the Truth, to your ignorance, and as the Life, to your mortality. He can do what you could not do for yourself, save you from your sins and restore you to the Father.

We sometimes miss that it is not loving to affirm someone in their waywardness; rather, love helps you to find your way. If someone is heading down a road where the bridge is out, is it exclusive to warn them and point them toward a safe crossing? Or, as a guy from church likes to say, "If the airplane is on fire there is nothing "exclusive" about pointing to the one exit."

---

183   Matthew 11:28-30.

PREPARING A PLACE

From bridges to airplanes, let's consider preparing a place.

> In my Father's house are many rooms. If it were not so, would I have told you that I go to prepare a place for you? [3] And if I go and prepare a place for you, I will come again and will take you to myself, that where I am you may be also.[184]

The difference between Christianity and other religions is who is doing the preparing.

Envision, newly expecting parents. When Amanda became pregnant with our daughter Hannah, I lost my workout room. Talk about priorities. I got moved to the basement so that the new arrival could be next to our bedroom. A place needed to be prepared before the new baby arrived. What kind of parents would we have been if we waited for Hannah to be born and welcomed this newborn by saying, "Go prepare yourself a place?" That would be ludicrous. Yet is that not the basis of most religions?

Every other religion requires you to do what you are unable to: prepare your own place. Whether through meditation, rituals, works, Five Pillars, Four Noble Truths, the Eight-Fold path, or making up for past wrongs, people are asked to prepare their own place by being good enough; however good enough may be defined. The problem is, how good is good enough? No matter how good you are, you can't undo the wrong you have done. You could always have done just a smidge better. There is no remedy for the sin that separates you from God. Jesus taught that He prepared the place for

---

184   John 14:2–3.

you with a hammer, nails, and a cross; His death on the cross is the atonement for your sin: a gift to be received by grace through faith.[185]

NOT HOW WELL YOU FOLLOW, BUT WHO

Jesus describes Himself as the way, not merely His teaching. His teaching is wise and guides you in how to live, but it is not about how well you follow, but Whom you follow. "No one comes to the Father except through me"[186] confronts two false ideas. First, I can rely on religion to get me to heaven. I have my checklist, if I only check all the right boxes. And second, that I can rely on my righteousness, that it is possible to check all the right boxes. Sometimes I hear, "Well surely so and so is in heaven, he or she was a good person." Good by what standard? I may look good compared to my neighbor, but what do I look like next to Jesus?

> ...if you try to build a highway to heaven with your own good works, you're building a toll road. You have to pay your own way as you go along, and you will run out of road long before you get to your destination because good is never good enough... because mere human goodness bypasses the cross of Christ and the grace of God.[187]

Religion operates with the premise, "I obey and so am accepted," whereas the gospel of Jesus operates by "I am

---

185   See Ephesians 2:1-10.
186   John 14:6.
187   Merritt, James. *God, I've Got a Question: Biblical Truth for Our Deepest Concerns.* Eugene, Oregon: Harvest House, 2011, p195.

accepted and so choose to obey." Christianity is first and foremost not about what you achieve, but Who you receive and what He achieved for you.

THE NECESSITY OF THE CROSS

If there were alternative paths to God, an idea that is foreign to most religions, not just Christianity, the death of Jevsus would be rendered unnecessary. What kind of God would send His Son to be crucified needlessly? If there are other options available, take one of those. It was the necessity of what Jesus achieved for you that eliminates alternate paths for coming to God; otherwise, you would have a sadistic, masochistic God Who enjoys suffering with no purpose. A God Who made Jesus suffer and die for no reason.

Thomas asked, "How do we know the way?" Jesus is the way through His death and resurrection. He is the truth in that He reveals the Father but also exposes your sin and need for forgiveness. He is the life in that through Him Who conquered death, you can receive life. The identity of Jesus is critical (chapters 6-10) to realizing why He is the way, the truth, and the life, and able to do for you what you could not do for yourself.

THE INESCAPABLE TRUTH

You can only know me to the extent that I reveal myself to you. What if I told one person that I am a Christian, turned around and told another that I was a Muslim, and to yet another that I was a Jew? You would accuse me of wearing masks, being schizophrenic, or suffering from multiple personalities. You would be left with no idea of knowing the real me.

If all the religions were true, then you are left with a God who wears masks, is schizophrenic, and suffers from multiple personalities. How can you know Who the true God is if you are presented with competing and contradictory claims regarding His nature and how He relates to you? Creation points you to the reality of God in general. Through the Scriptures and Jesus, God has made Himself known to you.

> If you had known me, you would have known my Father also. From now on you do know him and have seen him." [8] Philip said to him, "Lord, show us the Father, and it is enough for us." [9] Jesus said to him, "Have I been with you so long, and you still do not know me, Philip? Whoever has seen me has seen the Father. How can you say, 'Show us the Father'? [10] Do you not believe that I am in the Father and the Father is in me? The words that I say to you I do not speak on my own authority, but the Father who dwells in me does his works. [11] Believe me that I am in the Father and the Father is in me, or else believe on account of the works themselves. [188]

IT IS NOT ARROGANT IF IT IS TRUE

Jesus proclaims that nobody comes to the Father except through Him. But isn't that arrogant? Not if it is true. But it is offensive to some. At times the truth offends. If God has drawn and revealed the parameters for coming to Him, am I not arrogant to think I can choose a different way?

---

188   John 14:7–11.

At times, the truth offends; nonetheless, that doesn't make it any less true. I have been wrong occasionally, but that doesn't mean I enjoy hearing when I am. I have from time to time been cranky, said things I should not have said, and done things that I should not have done. I am thankful that I have people who love me enough to tell the truth to me when I go off the rails. You are not to live offensively; however, if you are honest, sometimes the truth will offend.

If the bridge is out ahead, I want someone who loves me enough to tell me even though I might be offended by being told I am heading the wrong way. Lee Strobel says it well,

> If Jesus was right about this, then he was being appropriately narrow minded. He was being like parents who are narrow enough to insist that their children walk on the sidewalk and not in the street, or a doctor who limits his prescription to medicine that will help rather than poison them, or the airline pilot who restricts his landing options to that narrow path to life called a runway...You see, we really want narrow approaches—as long as they are based on truth and points us in the direction that is best for us.[189]

Radical claims are only radical if you are unable to back them up. "Believe me that I am in the Father and the Father is in me, or else believe on account of the works themselves.[190] Jesus invites you to examine His words in light of His works. His claims, His life, and the fulfillment of prophecy, all put

---

189   Lee Strobel made this statement in a sermon or presentation titled "Jesus Is The Only Way To God? True OR False?"
190   John 14:11.

Him in a field of His own as part of the Trinity. The empty tomb confirms and validates that His claims are not empty but gives cause to believe them true.

Why Jesus in a world of so many alternatives? Because not all paths lead to the same destination. He is the way, the truth, and the life, and no one comes to the Father except through Him. He is the answer to the problem of sin for He provided the remedy through His death and resurrection. However, if Jesus is the only way, what about those who have never heard about Jesus?

Chapter 12

The Call to Believe

Romans 1:18-32

I was asked once to give my sermon in two minutes or less, so here you go. What about those who have never heard about Jesus? Well, they are not condemned for rejecting Jesus but for rejecting the truth available to them. What is fascinating is that those who use this question as a reason not to believe are those who have heard about Jesus and thereby left without excuse.

MISSING THE OBVIOUS

I read an illustration once about Sherlock Holmes and Dr. Watson going camping. They pitched their tent under the stars and went to sleep. Sometime in the middle of the night, Holmes wakes Watson. "Watson, look up at the stars and tell me what you deduce.' Watson says, "I see millions of stars, and if even a few of those have planets, it's quite likely that there are some planets like Earth, and if there are planets like Earth out there, there might also be life." Holmes replies, "Watson, you idiot, somebody stole our tent."

It is amazing how much you can see and yet miss the obvious. I suspect that all of you have at one time, or myriads of times, had the thought, "How did I miss that?" You are reading through the Scriptures again and wonder, "How did I not see that before?" Looking for your glasses only to realize they are sitting on your head. Pushing on a door that says, "Pull." We have all had moments when we missed the obvious.

On Memorial Day weekend, you celebrate and are reminded of those who laid down their lives for the freedom you, as an American, enjoy. One of the reasons you may lay out why Jesus is an appeal to the heart: He laid down His life for you. However, this book appeals to the mind, exploring reasons for belief. Hiding behind the question, "What about those who have never heard," is irrelevant for those who have.

With that said, it is an uncomfortable question raised by skeptics and believers alike, and which challenges our understanding of justice and fairness. When my daughter was young, she had a strong sense of what in her mind was fair. Only her outlook on fairness was limited to her perspective: fairness equals everyone having the same size slice of pie. Her viewpoint failed to account for all the details, such as what was free to her came at a cost to me. She was clouded by the limitations of how a young mind thinks. As you judge what is or isn't fair, whose lens are you looking through and are you considering the whole picture or just a slice of the pie?

THE SIMPLE MADE COMPLEX

How can God condemn someone for something they never had the opportunity to respond to? It is a hard question built on a wrong presupposition, but I will address that later. For now, let's take it at face value. Various ideas have been presented to attempt to alleviate the discomfort of the question. One such endeavor is to describe Jesus as ontologically necessary for salvation, but not epistemologically necessary. Say what? Now you see the kind of theological jargon I wade through for you. Simply put, this complex idea boils down to this: while the life, death, and resurrection of Jesus are essential for salvation, they can supposedly be effective without personal faith in Him. In other words, one could be saved by Jesus without ever knowing Him. While this view may ease the discomfort surrounding the fate of those who have never heard, it is not what Scripture—or Jesus Himself—taught.

Theologians can be guilty of looking at the stars and espousing complex theories while missing the truths right before their eyes. "Whoever believes in [Jesus] shall not perish",[191] all who call upon Him will be saved,[192] for there is One Mediator between God and man.[193] Watson, I believe we've found the tent! You may not understand the complex doctrines and nuances of Scripture that propel scholars into endless debate. Nevertheless, the matter of utmost importance is abundantly clear: the call to believe and the necessity of faith in Jesus for salvation.

WHAT IS FAIR?

It is not fairness, but by mercy and grace that anyone is saved. None of us deserve salvation. Paul lays out in Romans 1:18-3:23 the universal nature of sin culminating in the declaration, "for all have sinned and fall short of the glory of God".[194] Who

---

191 John 3:16.
192 Romans 10:8-13.
193 1 Timothy 2:5. These are just a few Scriptures of many highlighting the importance of your response to Jesus.
194 Romans 3:23.

falls under the category of falling short? All means all. God has given a means of salvation and that any are saved is not a matter of fairness or justice, but of His mercy and grace. We all deserve death, but as John Piper explains, "The wisdom of God devised a way for the love of God to deliver sinners from the wrath of God while not compromising the righteousness of God."[195] If you reject God's provision for sin in Jesus, that is upon you, not Him.

The Scriptures reveal that God is loving and just and that God desires for none to perish,[196] and that Jesus is the only way to life.[197] Yet there are a vast number of people who have never heard about Jesus. The argument goes, how is it loving, or just, to condemn those who have never heard? The biblical answer is that those who have never heard of Jesus are not condemned for rejecting Jesus, though that does not mean God is unjust in judging them. They are condemned based on what they did with what they could know.

NOTICING THE MISSING TENT

"For the wrath of God is revealed from heaven against all ungodliness and unrighteousness of men, who by their unrighteousness suppress the truth."[198] Where is God's wrath directed? Against ungodliness and unrighteousness. God's judgment is not capricious, arbitrary, or simply because you have never heard. No one is undeservedly judged simply because they never heard of Jesus, but because they have sinned and fallen short of the glory of God.[199] Once you eliminate

---

195   https://www.goodreads.com/quotes/371-the-wisdom-of-god-devised-a-way-for-the-love
196   2 Peter 3:9.
197   John 14:6.
198   Romans 1:18.
199   Romans 3:23.

God, you are left with a shaky foundation. Without God, there is no basis for morality. "Dostoyevsky reminded us in *The Brothers Karamazov* that 'if God does not exist, everything is permissible.' We are now seeing 'everything.' And much of it is not good to get used to."[200] This doesn't mean people are incapable of doing good. Rather, it highlights that they lack a logical foundation for defining or justifying goodness—and, of course, they don't always choose to do good.[201] But, who defines good? God doesn't grade on the curve, which is critical to know when it comes to judgment. It is not a matter of how we stack up to one another, but to a perfect and holy God. Since none of us measure up to perfection, we need a Savior who can accomplish what we never could on our own.

There is much in Romans 1:18-32 which I will not address in this chapter. I am not avoiding controversy, as the text is clear, however, my focus is on what about those who have never heard. Help me out here, God's wrath is revealed against what? Ungodliness and wickedness. Who has fallen short of the glory of God? All. The hard part for people to swallow is that "everyone deserves judgment" is our starting point.

SUPPRESSION OF TRUTH

How do you get from God created, and it was good[202] to ungodliness and wickedness? You can speculate and deduce elaborate theories, my dear Watson, or you can return to the text. "For the wrath of God is revealed from heaven against

---

200   Source: William J. Bennett, addressing the 20th anniversary celebration of the Heritage Foundation. Christianity Today, Vol. 38, no. 7.
201   The logical evolution of Darwin's theory is survival of the fittest. Philosophically, it only provides for self-serving to benefit oneself and offers no explanation for why people would truly serve one another. There is a sense of morality written on our hearts that evolution cannot explain.
202   Genesis 1:1-31.

all ungodliness and unrighteousness of men, who by their unrighteousness suppress the truth."[203] God has given you evidence for His existence through that which He created; evidence that people suppressed to replace the One true God with some god or gods of their making.[204]

The progression in Romans 1 is the regression that occurs through suppressing the truth about God. People today claim to be too sophisticated to bow before golden calves, Asherah poles, bronze serpents, etc. However, our culture has exchanged metal images for mental ones. Bowing before a false idea rather than an image is no less idolatrous. Creation serves as evidence for the existence of God. While everyone may not hear about Jesus, everyone does encounter the testimony and witness of God's creation.

> The heavens declare the glory of God, and the sky above proclaims his handiwork. [2] Day to day pours out speech, and night to night reveals knowledge. [3] There is no speech, nor are there words, whose voice is not heard. [4] Their voice goes out through all the earth, and their words to the end of the world. [205]

People are not accountable for what they cannot know but are culpable for the truth made known through creation, leaving them without excuse. Creation gives sufficient evidence to believe in God even if it is insufficient to point you more specifically to faith in Jesus. Those who have not heard about Jesus are not judged for rejecting Jesus but for suppressing the

---

203   Romans 1:18.
204   Romans 1:18-23.
205   Psalm 19:1–4.

truth that is available to them. Failing to honor God and give thanks to Him, leads to becoming futile in one's thinking and becoming fools for in essence they have exchanged the glory of God for a cheap fake, or today would we call it deepfake?[206] This is not a statement regarding people's IQ. Intelligent people can act foolishly. God has given you sufficient evidence to believe in and turn to Him but does not *force* you into believing. Once you begin the path of suppressing the truth, you claim to be wise but become a fool. I am doing my best not to dive into politically incorrect topics that reveal how foolish we have become in our time. Sam Storms astutely observes, "Clearly, then the person who rejects God does not cease to be religious. Indeed, he becomes religious in order to reject God. He substitutes for God a deity of his own making, often himself."[207] Remember that idolatry is not limited to metal images but extends to mental images or ideas, whatever you use to replace God.

IGNORANCE IS NO EXCUSE

If creation provides evidence for the Creator, then ignorance is not the lack of opportunity to know and supplies no excuse. Paul presents a deliberate refusal to accept what is before your eyes. Unfortunately, this applies not just to the unbeliever. To bring it painfully close to the believer, I have heard Christians comment: "I know I am living in sin," without any intent to address the sin they are living in, which is not ignorance but is ignorant.

---

206   Deepfake is highly realistic media generated by artificial intelligence that has manipulated reality.
207   Storms, Sam. *Tough Topics: Biblical Answers to 25 Challenging Questions.* Wheaten, Illinois: Crossway, 2013), p117.

The evidence of creation eliminates the excuse of ignorance for believing in God, but that does not give us sufficient revelation for believing in Jesus. It highlights that those who have not heard of Jesus are not judged for rejecting Jesus but for rejecting the Father, or the truth made available to them. Romans 1:24ff begins the logical conclusion of Romans 1:18-23 where the sin of suppressing the truth becomes part of the punishment. If you suppress the truth you know, then don't be surprised when you get what you get: the due penalty for doing so. Notice that God gave them up to what was already in them: shameful lusts, dishonorable passions, a depraved mind. God let them continue the path they had already chosen to walk. Condemned not for what they couldn't see but chose not to.

THOSE WHO ARE SEEKING, GOD HAS A WAY OF REACHING

If you have already rejected the truth you have been given, why is it upon God to add more truth to reject? On the flip side, when revelation is received, God provides the means for even greater understanding. "Where the word is not or cannot be preached by human agents, God is not inhibited from bringing people to faith in him, even if that act of hope and trust may lack the fully orbed character of an informed Christian faith."[208] For instance, if you listen regularly to Christian radio, you have likely heard that many Muslims come to faith in Jesus not through a Christian preacher but a dream or vision, giving a partial answer to what about those who have never heard.

---

208   McGrath, Alister. *Christian Theology: An Introduction.* Hoboken, New Jersey: Wiley-Blackwell, Fifth Edition, 2010.

The issue, then, is not whether or not you like this claim, but whether or not it is true. The usual smokescreen is to say, "What about those who have never heard of Jesus?" The response to this is twofold: (1) there is a missionary imperative in the New Testament to minimize this problem (that is why, for example, Paul dedicates his life to preaching Jesus where he has not yet been preached) and (2) how God may choose to reveal himself or deal with those who have no human messenger is his business. If we know God's character, we can trust him to do his business well.[209]

Acts 10 provides you with a good example of this with a Gentile by the name of Cornelius. When people respond positively to revelation, God gives more revelation, whether a dream, vision, messenger, or what have you. But if you reject revelation, God is not obligated to furnish more. This is true for the believer as well as the unbeliever. If you choose not to listen to the word you already know, then you should not be surprised by God's silence while seeking to hear His voice. Consider this illustration,

Let's suppose a friend telephones me and tells me he has just received two free tickets to a musical and wants to know if I would like to go. Since musicals do not interest me, I declined his kind offer. Now since I did not respond to his general invitation, he is under no obligation to

209   Kaiser, W. C., Jr., Davids, P. H., Bruce, F. F., & Brauch, M. T. (1996). *Hard sayings of the Bible* (p. 502). InterVarsity.

give me specifics pertaining to *which musical* is in town. For example, it would not have made any difference to me whether it was *Cats*, *Wicked*, or *A Chorus Line*. Now let's suppose instead that my friend had told me he had just received two free tickets to see a baseball game and wanted to know if I would like to go. Since I'm a baseball fan, I may ask him who's playing before accepting. In this case, since I responded to his general invitation, he will provide the specific details concerning the event.[210]

God has a way of reaching those seeking, but if you are not seeking, God is under no obligation to provide what you are not seeking.

WHAT ABOUT THOSE WHO DIED BEFORE JESUS

A related but different question is what about those who died before Jesus? Let's revisit an earlier passage.

Paul, a servant of Christ Jesus, called to be an apostle, set apart for the gospel of God, ² *which he promised beforehand through his prophets in the holy Scriptures*, ³ concerning his Son, who was descended from David according to the flesh ⁴ and was declared to be the Son of God in power according to the Spirit of holiness by

210   Licona, Michael. *Evidence for God: 50 Arguments for Faith from the Bible, History, Philosophy, and Science.* Ed by William A. Dembski and Michael R. Licona. Grand Rapids, Michigan: Baker Books, 2010, p196-197.

his resurrection from the dead, Jesus Christ our Lord,[211]

The gospel was promised beforehand through the prophets. Recall that whole thing about fulfilled prophecy (chapter 8). If you were to trace through Paul's argument you would eventually get to, "whom God put forward as a propitiation by his blood, to be received by faith. This was to show God's righteousness, because in his divine forbearance he had passed over former sins.[212] Our faith looks back to what Jesus accomplished, while theirs looked forward to the promise of what He would achieve.

The big picture is you are not judged for what you could not have known, but you are accountable for how you responded to what God has made available to you. Many who raise the question, "What about those who have never heard," are the same people refusing to respond to the knowledge made available to them. You cannot ask the question if you have not heard about Jesus and His claim to be the only way to the Father.

WHAT ABOUT THOSE UNABLE TO COMPREHEND

What about those without the mental capacity to comprehend the evidence of creation or the facts about Jesus? What about the mentally handicapped or young children, for instance? Looking back to the Old Testament precedent, who was

---

211   Romans 1:1–4.
212   Romans 3:25. Propitiation is the act of making something favorable, or in this case acceptable with the appeasing of justice. Our sins deserved judgment, but it was through Jesus' sacrifice that we can receive forgiveness through God's mercy and grace.

allowed to enter the Promised Land? Many of you may not know, others likely came up with two names, Joshua and Caleb. However, entry into the land was not limited to Joshua and Caleb. Joshua, Caleb, and the "little ones...who today have no knowledge of good and evil" were allowed to enter.[213] While the Bible doesn't directly answer this question, it strongly suggests that those without the mental capacity to understand—including young children—are not held accountable for what is beyond their grasp.[214]

THE CALL TO BELIEVE

With that said, you have read this book, thank you. You can grasp the information, and you have heard about Jesus. So now, dear reader, let's not miss the obvious. What matters to you is not how God may or may not handle those who have not heard, but with you who have. You and I are accountable for how we respond or fail to respond to Jesus. As Wallace put it at the end of his journey from atheism to faith,

> As you examine the evidence for Christianity, ask yourself the same question I eventually had to ask of myself: "Am I rejecting this because there isn't enough evidence, or am I rejecting this because I don't want there to be enough evidence?" Are you denying the resurrection on evidential grounds or simply because you are stubbornly biased against anything

---

213   Deuteronomy 1:34-39. Numbers 32:11 indicates that little ones included those up to 20 years old.

214   This also seems to be implied in David's statement in 2 Samuel 12:23 when his infant son had just died.

supernatural or pridefully unwilling to submit your authority?[215]

Are you suppressing the truth or seeking it? Are you giving God glory and thanks or offering it elsewhere? Are you honoring God through faith or giving yourself to what deep down, you know to be wrong? Why Jesus? Because "...I am not ashamed of the gospel, for it is the power of God for salvation to everyone who believes, to the Jew first and also to the Greek. [17] For in it the righteousness of God is revealed from faith for faith, as it is written, "The righteous shall live by faith."[216] You have the information at hand, will you answer the call to believe and walk in the obedience of faith for the sake of His name as one who belongs to Jesus?[217]

---

215   Wallace, J. W. (2014). Alive: a cold-case approach to the resurrection. David C Cook.

216   Romans 1:16–17.

217   Romans 1:5-6.

Acknowledgments

I thank my parents, Robert and JoAnn Jassman, for introducing me to Jesus, raising me in the faith, and setting me on the course of pursuing Him. I was blessed with my parents who guided me onto a good path.

I also thank my wife Amanda, who encouraged (and occasionally pushed) me in this endeavor and helped with proofreading and editing, along with Debbie Golden, Rich Irwin, and Anne Coleman who likewise provided feedback for my work.

I also need to acknowledge the many great scholars who preceded me and have been a part of my journey through their work, research, and writings, many of whom I have cited in this work. Their insights have nourished my faith and are reflected in this work, which has become a part of their legacy. I continue to pass on what has been handed down to me: the basis and rationale for believing. As Paul declares: "... that Christ died for our sins in accordance with the Scriptures, that he was buried, that he was raised on the third day in accordance with the Scriptures, and that he appeared to Cephas, then to the twelve",[218] and I am thankful that He has made Himself known to me.

---

218   1 Corinthians 15:3-5.

Author Bio

Pastor Dan Jassman began his ministry in 1996 with two small rural churches in Colfax and Arrowsmith, IL, where he also pursued his Master of Divinity graduating with high honors. He served these two churches for fourteen years and was led to move to Bloomington, IL, with his family to start a new church, Network Bible Fellowship, which officially launched in January of 2011. Dan continues to serve at Network Bible teaching God's word to equip His people to live out their faith in following Jesus. When God called Dan to the ministry, the calling was "to the people in the seats, not the streets," because he struggled with the reality that many Christians did not understand the faith they professed or what it truly meant to follow Christ. This conviction has fueled nearly thirty years of teaching the Bible in pastoral ministry, seeking to help people learn, grow, and live out their faith, including a year that was spent solely on apologetics and dealing with difficult scriptures and topics.

Dan is married to Amanda and has a daughter, Hannah, who has started her own family, blessing them with three grandchildren. He continues to pastor Network Bible Fellowship serving a congregation that values learning what the Bible teaches and discovering how biblical truth remains timeless and relevant in every generation. He remains committed to learning, deepening his understanding so he can teach more effectively as we grow together on this journey of following Jesus.

Visit Network Bible Fellowship at www.networkbible.org, or follow us on YouTube (@networkbiblefellowship1176) and Facebook.

URGENT PLEA!

Thank You for Reading My Book!

I really appreciate all of your feedback and
I love hearing what you have to say.

I need your input to make the next version of this
book (or any future books) better.

Please take two minutes now to leave a helpful review on
Amazon letting me know what you thought of the book.

Thanks so much!

- Dan Jassman

Made in the USA
Monee, IL
11 June 2025

19273911R00103